Godly Play

I wonder...

Graceful Nurture

Using Godly Play with Adults

Rebecca L. McClain

Church Publishing
NEW YORK

Church Publishing
19 East 34th Street
New York, NY 10016
www.churchpublishing.org

Cover design by Jennifer Kopec, 2Pug Design
Typeset by Progressive Publishing Services

Library of Congress Cataloging-in-Publication Data

A record of this book is available from the Library of Congress.

ISBN-13: 978-0-89869-967-8 (pbk.)
ISBN-13: 978-0-89869-968-5 (ebook)

Printed in Canada

Dedication

This offering is dedicated to my dear friend and colleague,
Jerome W. Berryman,
and to the memory of the beautiful Thea.

Graceful Nurture for Adults

An Invitation

Godly Play® is a treasure, and, in many ways, a best-kept secret. Many know Godly Play® as a Christian-education curriculum for children. They know it as a product to be considered and reviewed from among an array of choices available. Some are aware that it is Montessori based, and others know there is training available and resources to be purchased or crafted for the classroom. It is easy to see why few would consider Godly Play® as something else, and yet, that is exactly what I propose in this publication.

Godly Play® is not for children only—the method builds a spiritual framework for an integrated life—a life of action and contemplation, a life of communion and reflection. Godly Play® is a spiritual practice for all who are seeking a more graceful way of living.

From the mathematical equations of cosmology and quantum physics to the equally dense and complex world of neurobiology, all of Creation is built on a foundation of rhythmic patterns that flow toward integration and complexity. The spiral DNA that makes each of us unique in the world is the result of a pattern made up of four nucleotides. Imagine that you had just four letters with which to write and yet did so in a sequence so complex that all life on Earth, from the simplest to the most advanced, is formed. The reality of such a simple pattern translates into wonder.

And it is wonder that brings me to Godly Play®. The patterned rhythm of Godly Play® includes gathering in the circle, entering into a story, wondering, creating, sharing, and then being sent out on a spiritual pathway. The elegant simplicity of this spiral curriculum repeated over and over again changes participants, bringing a sense of peace and wholeness to each. And the gentle way we lean into each other in the circle, listening, offering, and sharing brings us home to the very hearth that made us a social species long ago. We are practicing being holy and being set apart for a more excellent use—an experience of the fullness of being "in Christ." Theologically, we might speak of a soulful life; neurologically, we are experiencing an integration of bodily systems into a complex and cohesive whole. We are one.

This practice of Godly Play® is a balm to the chaotic and divided lives we experience much of the time. Many who come to the church are overwhelmed and wounded by their pace of life, the lack of balance, and the loss of community. The separate states of chaos and rigidity are sources of disintegration. But when adults begin to experience this simple pattern of being together, something changes. They know grace, and they experience the wonder of integration and flow— deeply connected within and without. Godly Play® offers us this way of grace and sets us on a journey home.

I invite you to join me in this journey. I believe we are just beginning.

Come and see,
The Very Rev. Rebecca L. McClain

Contents

Preface xi

Getting Ready 1

Essentials 3

Lesson Planning 11

Overview of the Stories 17

Course I

The Heavenly Banquet (Preparation for Baptism,
Confirmation, and Reaffirmation of Vows)

.... 19

Designed for twelve weeks with ninety-minute lessons

Desired Outcome 20

Room, Materials, and Resources 21

Lesson 1: Circle of the Church Year 22

Lesson 2: Creation 26

Lesson 3: The Great Family 29

Lesson 4: The Exodus 31

Lesson 5: The Exile and the Return 32

Lesson 6: The Holy Family 34

Lesson 7: Advent and Christmas 36

Lesson 8: Parable of the Good Shepherd 39

Lesson 9: The Faces of Easter I–VII 40

Lesson 10: Knowing Jesus in a New Way 42

Lesson 11: The Greatest Parable 44

Lesson 12: Baptism, the Good Shepherd, and World Communion 46

Course II

Dessert Only (Preparation for Families Beginning Godly Play®) 49

Designed for six weeks with sixty-minute lessons

Desired Outcome 50

Room, Materials, and Resources 50

Lesson 1: Circle of the Church Year 51

Lesson 2: The Great Family 53

Lesson 3: The Holy Family 55

Lesson 4: Parable of the Good Shepherd 56

Lesson 5: The Faces of Easter I–VII 57

Lesson 6: Baptism 59

Course III

Slow Cooking (Retreat) 61

Designed for a day and a half with ninety-minute lessons

Desired Outcome 61

Room, Materials, and Resources 63

Lesson 1: Circle of the Church Year 63

Lesson 2: Creation 65

Lesson 3: The Great Family 68

Lesson 4: The Holy Family 69

Lesson 5: Parable of the Good Shepherd 70

Lesson 6: Baptism, the Good Shepherd, and World Communion 72

Course IV

Coffee with Cream (Sunday Mornings) 75

Designed for twelve weeks with forty-five-minute lessons

Desired Outcome 75

Room, Materials, and Resources...76

Lesson 1: Circle of the Church Year 76

Lesson 2: Creation 78

Lesson 3: The Great Family 80

Lesson 4: The Exodus 82

Lesson 5: The Exile and the Return 83

Lesson 6: The Holy Family...84

Lesson 7: Advent and Christmas 86

Lesson 8: Parable of the Good Shepherd 87

Lesson 9: The Faces of Easter I–VII..88

Lesson 10: Knowing Jesus in a New Way...89

Lesson 11: The Greatest Parable..91

Lesson 12: Baptism 92

Bibliography 95

Additional Resources 96

Authors and Other Sources of Inspiration 96

Appendix: Sample Materials 99

Preface

> At that time the disciples came to Jesus and asked, "Who is the greatest in the kingdom of heaven?" He called a child, whom he put among them, and said, "Truly I tell you, unless you change and become like children, you will never enter the kingdom of heaven. Whoever becomes humble like this child is the greatest in the kingdom of heaven. Whoever welcomes one such child in my name welcomes me."
>
> —Matthew 18:1–5

An Invitation

After thirty years of working with adults who are entering or returning to church, I have come to believe that Godly Play® is the most graceful way to nurture the children of God of every age. This book offers a sampling of lesson plans to be used with adults in short courses of six to twelve weeks. The material is also excellent for use in retreats, preparation for baptism, and confirmation and reaffirmation of vows. Ultimately, our goal is the same for all ages: *the art of knowing how to use the language of the Christian people to make meaning about life and death and find direction for daily living.*[1] In other words, Godly Play® is an integrated and holistic model of Christian living for every age and stage of life.

In this book, we will discuss the challenges of creating safe spaces for adults, a way of issuing the invitation to become like a child while simultaneously acknowledging their years and experiences. Each of the four offered courses contains suggestions for helping adults fully participate and experience the freedom that is inherent in children.

The eight volumes of *The Complete Guide to Godly Play* and the primer *Teaching Godly Play* are foundational sources of information for all four of these courses. The volume of research in Dr. Berryman's fifty-five year pursuit of the question of the spirituality of the child is unparalleled in its quality and depth, and continues to this day. As the leading scholar on the topic of the spirituality of the child,

---

[1] Berryman, *The Complete Guide to Godly Play*, Vol. 8–9.

Dr. Berryman guides us along a pathway of incredible wisdom, drawing on the breadth and depth of scholars in the diverse fields of theology, scripture, history, liturgy, spirituality, poetry, pedagogy, creativity, sociology, developmental psychology, neurobiology, linguistics, social intelligence, emotional intelligence, and the arts. Yet all the theory and study in the world cannot take the place of sitting in the circle with children; in Godly Play® every story has been shaped in the company of children. Dr. Berryman has studied and played, observed, practiced, and wondered in the company of children of all ages, offering to the world a way of being human that transcends mere method—Godly Play® opens our hearts and minds to abundant life, if only we are willing to become like children.

This is the beginning of an important conversation that has wondrous implications for our life together in Christ.

Adult Theological Re-education

Many of the adults in our ministries lack an in-depth language of the heart, as Marcus Borg notes in his lecture, "Two Visions of Christianity Today":

> Adult theological re-education at the congregational level is an urgent need within American churches today. It is essential to Christian formation. And from my own experience and from a number of studies, I know that it has been a source of re-vitalizations in hundreds of congregations around the country.[2]

Robert Capon also reminds us of the "heart language" in *The Astonished Heart*:

> In our modern, Western way of looking at ourselves, we locate the intellect in the head and the emotions in the heart; but the ancient Jews had a different schema. For them, it was the heart with which they thought—remember "the thoughts and intents of the heart?"

---

[2] "OREGON: Marcus Borg named canon theologian at Trinity Cathedral in Portland." *Episcopal News Service*.

And it was the kidneys of all things with which they felt—"my heart and my reins trouble me in the night season." And we cannot forget "the bowels of compassion," that feeling in our gut. They understood the fullness of humanity.[3]

Neuroscientists now know what the Hebrew people long ago expressed: We as human beings are a psychosomatic unity—our body and soul are indivisible:

> The body is an essential part of how the mind functions. As we've seen, we can define a core aspect of the mind as an embodied and relational process that regulates the flow of energy and information.[4]

While the church is adept at explanatory and knowledge-based education for adults (direct instruction), it has often been less effective at delivering affective, expressive formation programs. Creating an interactive spiritual formation for members of Generation X and for Millennials is critically important, for many of them have little or no experience with the language of the Christian people.

Researchers note that the percentage of unchurched people in Generation X and amongst Millennials is between sixty-five and seventy percent and even among the churched, attendance is falling significantly. C. Kirk Hadaway reports that as many as eighty percent of Protestants and seventy-two percent of Catholics are essentially unchurched, attending less than once a month. This changing cultural reality has left many without the vocabulary of faith or knowledge of the Biblical narrative.

In response to this gloomy forecast, Diana Butler Bass in *Christianity After Religion: The End of the Church and the Birth of a New Spiritual Awakening*, offers a more hopeful future as she describes The Fourth Great Awakening.

---

[3] Capon, *The Astonished Heart*, 119.

[4] Siegel, *The Pocket Guide to Interpersonal Neurobiology*, 78.

Romantic realism begins with the self-in-relationship, not the iso-lated here, but the individual whose life is linked with other heroic lives in a quest for beauty and justice and love. Romantic realism is strengthened through spiritual practices that shape devotion, character, and ethics. These practices require attention, time, and teaching; they need to be formed and nurtured in a guild-like community of beginners, novices, craftspeople, masters, and innovators.[5]

Godly Play® embodies this approach to a spiritual life, especially among those who are seeking a more authentic path to God.

The method of Christian formation in many settings has been and still is more aligned with a "rational worldview emanating from the Enlightenment."[6] Many mainline progressive Christians are fond of saying, "I belong to the thinking person's church." This oft-repeated phrase fits nicely with the adult Sunday school curriculum of the 1950s and 1960s. Now, however, in the post-modern, post-Christian era, the Church must engage adults of all ages with the means and practices of how to experience the divine, ask transformational ques-tions, and encounter our world with meaningful solutions.

I learned a great deal about God and the Church in Sunday school but came to *know* God from my experience in worship and my pas-sion for the natural world. As a child of the 1950s, I was allowed to run free and encounter the glory of God in Creation unfiltered by anx-ious, hovering parents. And I was fortunate to come of age in a parish that welcomed young children in the worship services. I learned to chant, to sing the great hymns and anthems, to hear the beautiful poetry of psalms and canticles of the morning and evening offices, and to experience in my very bones the sensory delight of this sacred space. I realize now that I learned to play with God in the rhythm of worship—my own spirit was nurtured sufficiently to keep me at the table through adolescence and adulthood. That was not the case for many of my generation, and successive generations have fared worse.

---

[5] Bass, *Christianity After Religion*, 239.

[6] Robinson, *Out of Our Minds*, 106.

Why Godly Play® for Adults?

This little book is written to help church leaders engage adults in the transformational stories of Godly Play® in scripture and tradition through the curious, wondering questions of a child. Clergy and lay leaders are responsible for the spiritual formation of adults and children but often have little exposure or training in educational practices. I believe that the special challenge of adult faith formation today is primarily one of language development through the integration of story and experience. As adults, we may know the words of the Christian tradition, but all too often, we lack the context and frame of the language of the scriptural narrative. Stories provide the context so that we are able to make meaning of the words in our own lives. Godly Play® offers a new way for adults to enter more fully into life together in Christ.

The Rev. Dr. Jerome W. Berryman has created a model for lifelong formation, an experience that renews, refreshes, reframes, and restores the soul. I think it is a secret too good to keep from the beautiful child that dwells in each of us. To release the child within is not to deny a lifetime of living, but to integrate that life, infusing it with meaning, purpose, and direction. A friend recently wrote, "In the church we often over-teach and under-train in faith communities. In our symbol-driven realm, I would also say that we tend to overthink and under-experience." We leap to systematic symbolic language—defining words like *faith, grace, peace,* and *salvation*—forgetting the stories that bring these words alive.

I am also aware that many adults come to the church lacking even the most basic vocabulary of the Christian faith. Others arrive at our doorstep weighed down with the theological language of guilt and shame. Still others are victims of arrested spiritual development and insufficient skills to integrate their faith with their day-to-day life. In our enthusiasm to share the richness of our own traditions, we often begin in the middle of our story, assuming a common language and an ability to engage in God-talk. The ground has not been prepared, the foundation has not been laid, and, all too often, the seeker is quickly disillusioned and disenfranchised. I wonder how many slip away, bewildered?

For too long, we have believed that adult conversation and conversion starts with thoughtful theological discourse, biblical scholarship, and a short course in the history of the Christian people. Ken Robinson calls this the *rationalist approach,* and it has dominated much of educational theory (and for that matter, seminary education) for centuries and still shapes much of adult formation today.[7]

In the case of those seeking refuge from rigid fundamentalism, the rationalist approach has been a godsend and should not be discarded. Marcus Borg was a great champion, calling us into a rich and healthy understanding of our faith and clearly articulating the importance of fluency. Education for Ministry (EFM) and other similar curricula and tools are wonderful for those whose formation has been long and loving. But, often, we are working with those who have no foundation at all. And, there, the rationalist approach is not sufficient to transform the heart, to open the imagination, and to integrate the whole person to a full and expressive life in Christ. It also fails to satisfy our deep need for connection, the need to abide in the shelter of each other.

The world's leading social biologist, Edward O. Wilson, claims, "We are devoted to stories because that is how the mind works—a never-ending wandering through past scenarios and through alternative scenarios of the future."[8]

Stories are not just for children; it is through storytelling that identity is shaped, relationships are developed, and a future is imagined. The vocabulary of story is visual, aural, and sensual; it activates the mind/body connection. "Taste and see that the Lord is good," we proclaim in Psalm 34:8, and our minds race through a symbolic energy flow pattern, free association, remembering, and imagining. I wonder what *you* see, taste, and remember. Spiritual formation is shaped by such moments as we open up to each other, the great stories provoking and evoking our own experiences.

Language was the grail of human social evolution, achieved. Language is not basic; it is derived. We believe that it actually derives from the uniquely human abilities to read and share intentions with other people—which also underwrite other uniquely human skills that

[7] Robinson, *Out of Our Minds*, 1996.
[8] Wilson, *The Meaning of Human Existence*, 318.

emerge along with language such as declarative gestures, collaboration, pretense, and imitative learning.[9] To consider the possibility that language exists only because of our social nature calls into question the often-repeated statement of Descartes, "I think therefore I am." In one sense, there is no "I" outside of the context of "we." Blaise Pascal was much more attuned to our true reality: "The heart has its reasons, which reason knows not." We are neither disembodied nor disconnected thinkers but, more accurately, social beings that are tethered together body and soul. Our hearts beat as one! Godly Play® allows us to bring our current context (this time and this space) alongside the biblical narrative in a way that prepares us for a fully integrated life as *hoi adelphoi* (brothers and sisters).

What has been lost in this post-enlightenment, post-rational, and post-modern world is this amazing neurological truth:

> The mind is both embodied in an internal physiological context and embedded in an external relational context. Embodied and embedded is the fundamental nature of mind and this process regulates the flow of energy and information.[10]

Godly Play® is uniquely designed to hold this dynamic tension as we move through the experience of gathering, storytelling, wondering, working, Feasting, and being sent out.

The language of the Christian people is derived, expressive, embodied, and embedded, and it allows us to remember who we are, where we have been, and finally to imagine where we are going. Without fluency, we are lost, we are unable to tell our story, and we cannot imagine our future. I believe this is a fundamental problem in the church today—we are adept in talking about God, but we do not know the language of God. We cast about using the languages we know: marketplace, economics, business, law, science, psychology, philosophy, politics, technology, and every other language domain in which we are facile, desperately seeking to save the Church. What we have lost is the pure joy and astonishment of the story we tell.

---

[9] Wilson, *The Social Conquest of Earth*, 328.
[10] Siegel, *The Pocket Guide to Interpersonal Neurobiology*, xxvi.

Even theology fails us; for when language becomes increasingly abstract and symbolic, we begin to lose the mind-body connection. We are disembodied, talking heads. Godly Play® takes us back to the ground, calls for the evocative experience of sight, sound, touch, smell, and taste. We are reborn, reintegrated human beings who begin to feel connected with each other, the earth, the self, and God. It is the beginning of a more soulful way of living that is not detached, but it is integrated into the very mystery and rhythm of life, where wonder and play become the domain of all.

This work of fostering a conversion of the heart translates into patterns of behavior that reshape and reform the faith community from intellectual assent to empathetic action. We rediscover this deep truth:

> Human beings are enmeshed in social networks. From infancy we are predisposed to read the intention of others, and quick to cooperate if there is even a trace of shared interest. We are inclined to instinctive empathy and cooperation.[11]

Conversations and conversions must begin in the heart, reclaiming this deeply nurturing way of being together. Equipping adults through the experience of the nurturing circle of Godly Play® allows the language of the Christian people to unfold through the *Sacred Stories, Liturgical Action, Parables,* and *Silence.* It is here where adults can also become fluent and find meaning. It is here where we recover our true selves and can experience new life.

At the heart of it all, we discover that we need each other more than we could ever have imagined. Most people assume that the body they inhabit is self-regulating—that their own physiological balance occurs within a "closed loop," but what we have discovered is very different. We are wired together, "dependent on a system of interactive coordination wherein steadiness comes from synchronization with nearby attachment figures."[12] Simply put: we are one.

The consequences of this social aspect of our humanity are enormous. We cannot engage in the practice of spiritual formation without

---

[11] Wilson, *The Social Conquest of Earth,* 226.

[12] Lewis, Amini, and Lannon, *A General Theory of Love,* 84.

the explicit intention of creating a communal experience. And that work demands the kind of guidance that comes from leaders aware of and equipped to support this exquisite limbic connection.

And if we can experience rebirth (individually and socially), we can also recover our capacity to act. Parker Palmer writes eloquently in *An Active Life*, about this kind of expressive action that is born from such a life. Recovering the original restored and renewed vision of being human offers the promise that we might again be seen as living signs of God's love in the world.

Church Growth

We know from extensive research projects on the current climate of our churches that many of congregations are not growing, but this same research notes that the top three priorities in every congregation are tied to growth in numbers and in depth of spirituality. From *Holy Cow Consulting*, Russ Crabtree reports that these three priorities include the following:

1. Make necessary changes to attract families with children and youth to our church.

2. Develop and implement a comprehensive strategy to reach new people and incorporate them into the life of the church.

3. Move decisively to provide high quality education for every age and stage of life.[13]

We say we want to grow numerically and spiritually, but we continue to approach adult faith formation through the rationalist traditions. R.D. Laing said that this perspective "represses not only the instincts, but any form of transcendence."[14] This failure to create a culture of life-long learning has been at the heart of the existential crisis that emerged in the twentieth century and continues to plague our world today. It is time for a more holistic approach to formation where the very form of the work gives shape, coherence, and meaning to our lives. Godly Play® serves as a primer for Christian living,

[13] Crabtree, *Owlsight*, 89.
[14] Robinson, *Out of Our Minds*, 122.

grounding us in the stories, ritual action, and mystery that comes with consciousness. We remember who we are.

The elaboration of culture depends upon long-term memory, and in this capacity, humans rank far above all animals. The vast quantity stored in our immensely enlarged forebrains makes us consummate storytellers. We summon dreams and recollections of experience from across a lifetime and use them to create scenarios, past and future. We live in our conscious mind with the consequence of our actions, whether real or imagined. Played out in alternative versions, our inner stories allow us to override immediate desires in favor of delayed pleasure. By long-range planning we defeat, for a while at least, the urging of our emotions. This inner life is why each person is unique and precious. When one dies, an entire library of both experience and imaginings is extinguished.[15] Yet, we can be elevated to a life of meaning and purpose, as we hold these precious stories within the frame of the language of faith, finding hope even in the face of death.

Fluency in the Language of the Christian People

We assume adults are sufficiently grounded in the language of faith to engage in a spiritual conversation in their faith communities, though many have been formed in settings where a common language was not shaped at all or came through the lens of other doctrinal and theological perspectives. We know Godly Play® provides that foundational language for children, but I have discovered it can also help adults construct the language for themselves as they journey through their own stages of spiritual maturation so that they, too, become "co-creators in the biological, psychological, social and spiritual spheres of life."[16]

Godly Play® is about the acquisition of the language of the Christian people so that they might be equipped to make meaning in and of their lives. The culture of the Church holds the stories that form us for abundant life. The recovery of this story-driven language will quicken

---

[15] Wilson, *The Social Conquest of Earth*, 213, 214.

[16] Berryman, *The Complete Guide to Godly Play*, Vol. 2, 35.

our worship, strengthen our communal life together, and empower us to leap with joy in our world.

Robert Capon wonderfully rehearses the history of the Church in *The Astonished Heart,* ending with these words:

> Resurrection reigns wherever there is death; and with it comes the joy of the really Good News: the dance into the New Creation in Christ will always be alive and well. Desire, however we manage it, can always explode into astonishment.[17]

It is this story that will pull us into a more wondrous future.

---

[17] Capon, *The Astonished Heart,* 122.

Getting Ready

Now there was a Pharisee named Nicodemus, a leader of the Jews. He came to Jesus by night and said to him, "Rabbi, we know that you are a teacher who has come from God; for no one can do these signs that you do apart from the presence of God." Jesus answered him, "Very truly, I tell you, no one can see the kingdom of God without being born from above. Nicodemus said to him, "How can anyone be born after having grown old? Can one enter a second time into the mother's womb and be born?" Jesus answered, "Very truly, I tell you, no one can enter the kingdom of God without being born of water and Spirit."

—John 3:1–5

Godly Play® allows for introspection for the sake of the soul and extroversion for the sake of the community. The wondering and work invites each participant to cross their own threshold into mystery and meaning. The circle becomes the nest, the place where our social nature is nourished, where we come home. Godly Play® offers a methodology that builds upon the concept of developing a spiral from the heart to the head and back again. This foundational language is presented through the simplicity of the biblical narrative and the invitation to enter the story at a deeper level. It is here where the real work of a life of faith begins for disciples of all ages.

It is my hope to begin a conversation with leaders charged with the care of the souls of adults. We begin with awareness that the Church has forgotten the admonition of Jesus to become like children. Through Godly Play®, we prepare adults to be born again, remembering the invitation of Jesus to Nicodemus. Only then can they learn to place themselves within the biblical narrative and begin to ask the deeper questions, questions that are different at every stage of life. Jerome Berryman often says that to be equipped with the language of the Christian people means to be steeped in the stories of the biblical narrative, to be centered within the context of the *Liturgical Action*, to enter into the mysterious realm of the parabolic and to learn to rest the soul in the silence of wonder.

There are many ways to nurture an adult community using Godly Play®. I propose four courses, each uniquely nourishing:

- Course I: The Heavenly Banquet (Preparation for Baptism, Confirmation, and Reaffirmation of Vows)
- Course II: Dessert Only (Preparation for Families Beginning Godly Play®)
- Course III: Slow-Cooking (Retreat)
- Course IV: Coffee and Cream (Sunday Mornings)

Godly Play® Method

It is my hope that our readers will already be practitioners of the Godly Play® method. If you are not, there are excellent resources, trainings, and Storytellers in many faith communities all around the world. Guidance can be found in *The Complete Guide* and *Teaching Godly Play,* both by the Rev. Dr. Jerome W. Berryman. Our hope is that clergy leaders and professional educators will become fluent in the Godly Play® method as an essential part of their own formation. There is simply no substitute for great training.

Most of all, it is just as important to become fluent in the Godly Play® method when working with adults as it is with children. Working with a skilled Storyteller is a very good option if you are not yet trained; Storytellers will be honored to share this gift with adults.

Opportunities to become more familiar with the method can be found in the written materials, stories posted on the Godly Play® YouTube site and training events, all available at the Godly Play® website, www.godlyplay.org. Materials and books are available through the Godly Play® website from Godly Play® Resources in Ashland, Kansas. *The Complete Guide, Teaching Godly Play,* and other print materials written by Dr. Berryman are also available in print at https://www.churchpublishing.org/complex/godlyplayprint/ and digitally at https://www.churchpublishing.org/complex/godlyplaydigital/ from Church Publishing Incorporated (https://www.churchpublishing.org). In this particular book, only a few Godly Play® stories will be told, but you are limited only by your imagination. This is just the beginning of a conversation.

Essentials

First Things

It is essential to be prepared for each Godly Play® class. No matter the setting, there should be a Storyteller and a Doorperson. The Storyteller and Doorperson work together, including preparing the space for participants. The stories found in *The Complete Guide* (in either print or digital versions) are noted in the Overview of the Stories on pages 17–18. Each lesson provides not only the story but also a wealth of relevant information and insight. Being ready begins with the leaders always ensuring that provision has been made for the Feast and materials are available for the work. In Course I, participants provide for the Feast after the first two lessons. Each of the four course options brings special needs with regard to space and pace. Please be mindful of which story or stories will be used so that you are ready, too.

The Complete Guide has everything you need to tell the stories. *Teaching Godly Play* provides a wonderful overview of the method and rationale. Preparation is key. The rest of this book contains lesson plan pages for each course as well as notes, thoughts, and ideas to develop your plans for your group. Each group will be a little different, and the experience will emerge in different ways, so this is an opportunity for boundaried creativity. The stories are complete, the wondering is there, and the work can be creatively approached. There is a bibliography at the end (pp. 95–97) that contains additional resources that may be useful, especially for the study time in Course I.

Gathering

When the children come to the Godly Play® space, the Doorperson welcomes them at the door. They say goodbye to their parents and are welcomed by name into the room. The Storyteller invites each child to join the circle, and when all are present and ready, the Storyteller begins. Adults also need to be welcomed at the door, invited to cross the threshold, and encouraged to join the Storyteller in the circle. In the beginning of our courses, we will have a slightly different rhythm described in more detail in each lesson plan overview. Two things continue to be important: *being welcomed by name* and *being invited into the circle*. Then, we "get ready."

Getting Ready

In Godly Play®, children are encouraged to ready themselves; adults may need a little more help. When all participants have gathered, the Storyteller invites everyone to get in a comfortable position—either in a chair or on the floor—and to close their eyes. For a minute or two, all are invited to breathe deeply, in and out. Breathing deeply brings oxygen into the body, lowering anxiety, releasing the tension we hold onto in our bodies all the way down to the cellular level. This is also a way to help participants shift into a different kind of learning mode. Throughout this series of lessons, we will follow a similar pattern of getting ready for our story. It will get easier, and we will get better at forming a good circle. More information on gathering and getting ready will be found in the first lesson.

Telling the Story

Dr. Berryman says, "The presentations describe an integration of action, words, and teaching artifacts for each lesson. The *Sacred Stories*, *Parables*, *Liturgical Action*, and *Contemplative Silence* are presented as tools to make meaning."[18]

The Wondering

The Godly Play® presentation invites the participants to generate meaning from the interplay between their life experiences and the story.[19]

At first, the wondering may feel awkward. Adults often think that there must be correct answers or perhaps that there is a trick to this wondering. Silence can be unbearable. The Storyteller must

---

[18] Berryman, *Teaching Godly Play*, 40.
[19] Berryman, *Teaching Godly Play*, 41.

breathe and let the silence continue until someone is brave enough to respond. The good news is that participants get better and better at their wondering. Sir Kenneth Robinson tells us, "Imagination is the primary gift of human consciousness. In imagination, we can step out of the here and now. We can take a different view of the present by putting ourselves in the mind of others: we can try to see with their eyes and feel with their hearts."[20] This is the nature of wondering and what makes Godly Play® so very different in shaping one for Christian living.

The Complete Guide and *Teaching Godly Play* provide the process for reflection and wondering. Know the story for each lesson and thoroughly review the supplemental material from *The Complete Guide*. There are four "genres" (or types of stories) in Godly Play®:

- *Sacred Stories*
- *Liturgical Action*
- *Parables*
- *Silence*

The Work

From Sir Kenneth Robinson, we learn that our current education models have often stifled the creative spirit.[21] Asking five-year-olds if they can dance, draw, or sing brings squeals of delight: "Of course we can dance! Of course we can draw! And paint! And sing! Watch us!" I have found inviting adults into such activities leads to awkward silences or excuses why they couldn't possibly participate. The wondering was hard enough, but this work is too much. Robinson also explains, "Creativity is a step further on from imagination. Creativity does. Creativity involves putting your imagination to work. Being creative involves doing something, creativity is applied imagination."[22]

---

[20] Robinson, *Out of Our Minds*, 141.

[21] Robinson, "Do Schools Kill Creativity?".

[22] Robinson, *Out of Our Minds*, 142.

Many approaches in Christian formation (especially with adults) bypass imagination and go directly to information. We teach and learn about the church, we study the content of Holy Scripture, our history, theology, and liturgy. Even in our practice of meditation and prayer, the work is focused on "how" to do something. This is the realm of "systematic" symbols, but it is not the *work* of Godly Play®. That work follows the story and the wondering is interior, integrative, and responsive. We release the imagination and wondering to act in response to the whole pattern of ideas simultaneously. We move formation from the realm of "systematic" symbols to "schematic" symbols.[23]

Systematic symbols, such as letters or numbers, are words intended to define or explain, or they are numbers used as a measure of time and place. They are often what we rely on in adult formation. Schematic symbols are discovered in paintings, poems, music, dance, and they are found in architecture or patterns in the natural world. "Their meanings are uniquely expressed in the forms they take." Schematic symbols can use systematic symbols—poetry for example—but again, meaning is expressed in the form, not the explanation.[24] I would contend that scripture can also be approached as schematic symbol, meaning expressed in the form of sacred texts. In fact, to see *Sacred Stories, Liturgical Action, Parables,* and *Silence* approached in this way is deeply rewarding, shaping the whole person for a life of meaning. We are engaged in a formative model of learning that anchors the experience in the long-term memory centers of the brain.

In the Age of Enlightenment and Reason, a shift occurred in the way in which we approached faith development, especially through the lens of scripture. The modern critical method focused on scripture as systematic symbol: rather than finding meaning expressed in the form of these sacred texts, we began to focus on defining words, confirming dates, and authenticity of time and place. From the quest for the historical Jesus to the Jesus Seminar, this mode has dominated academic circles and been key to adult formation in many faith

---

[23] Robinson, *Out of Our Minds*, 147–150.
[24] Robinson, *Out of Our Minds*, 147–150.

communities. Too often, rejection of this critical approach has resulted in a literal interpretation of the systematic symbols, creating a deep divide among faith communities—we find ourselves labeled either liberal or literal. What may be more helpful today is to recover the experience of scripture as schematic symbol, finding meaning is expressed in the very shape of the sacred texts.

In Godly Play®, meaning *is* expressed in the form. Godly Play® is not simply telling the stories of the Bible to the children as if systematic symbols have the power to transform. The whole enterprise of Godly Play® in its very structure and shape is about schematic symbols. Our tools— *Sacred Stories, Liturgical Action, Parables,* and *Silence*—activate the spiritual quest for meaning. Our work is not about the cataloging of details, rehearsing content, or discerning the correct understanding. Our work is our response to an encounter with a deep longing for purpose and meaning, our existential quest to know and be known and to be fluent in this language.

Young children have little trouble with this shift; after the story and the wondering, they are sent off to do their work. They are surrounded with opportunities. Stories, art supplies, and a room filled with things that are for them unleash their creativity. Adults will often move from wondering to anxiety: I don't know what to do. I don't know how to draw or paint or write poetry. We help participants rediscover their creativity. We liberate their hearts and minds, helping them to integrate their responses to the story so they become fluent in the language of the Christian people. Unlike children who are developmentally and physiologically primed for this work, many, if not most, adults have been exiled from their imaginations, compartmentalized in their thinking, and at sea with the freedom to respond without the ever watching eye of judgment. A wonderful resource to spark creativity in adults is the book *Awakening the Creative Spirit: Bringing the Arts to Spiritual Direction* by Christine Valters Painter and Betsey Beckman.[25]

With a little guidance, creativity can be unleashed, even from adults who don't believe they can dance, draw, or sing. For those who are already liberated, release them; for those who are unsure about

---

[25] Painter and Beckman, *Awakening the Creative Spirit.*

what to do, provide a few provocative materials. As you prepare your response materials, select paintings, photographs, or visual images or objects that speak to the lessons. (See the appendix for samples). With those who are struggling to respond, here is a list of thoughts and questions that may spark imagination:

- First, help them return to their breath; just two minutes of breathing and releasing extraneous thoughts is enough to activate a shift to a more mindful state.

- Describe what you see or feel.

- What is triggered in you?

- Connect this experience with someone or something in your life.

- Create a simple haiku with these words (5-7-5 syllables).

- Select a photograph or drawing that triggers something from your experience of the story.

- Using the materials provided, capture this experience so you might remember.

Remind participants that there is no wrong way for them to be creative. In the creative world, *no one gets hurt*, and, like children, adults also need nonevaluative and empowering questions and comments in response to their work.

The Feast

After the work, we gather again in our circle for the Feast. It is a rich—and sometimes quiet—time, a time to return to the nest to be nourished and to nourish. Here we become part of the Great Family. We recommend that this schedule not conflict or overlap with regular mealtimes. Mornings, afternoons, or evenings are perfect with the Feast as a foretaste of the heavenly banquet. The timing allows participants to fully participate in the experience without the distraction and business of a big meal, but it does not mean that our Feast will be mean and spare. In this program, we are going to explore the richness of small things. In *Supper of the Lamb*, Robert Capon says,

"One can do worse than be poor. He can miss altogether the sight of the greatness of small things."[26] Our small Feast will be something to savor. Be creative in choosing special food and drink, even if offering just one bite or sip. Take time to eat and drink mindfully. This part of our gathering differs from the children's version in this way: we are well-schooled in the rhythm of the Eucharistic feast, but we often suffer from a distorted orientation regarding food. We need to practice the joy of the Feast that is meant to be savored—this is about living an abundant life, even in the small things. In the spirit of the Feast as experienced by the children, adult participants take turns preparing and serving the food and drink. Even though the meal is small, it is a chance to share something special.

Godly Play®, like worship, is a valuing activity. The root word for worship in Old English is *weorthscipe*, a condition of being worthy, of affirming worth. The object of worth is God.

Our question is always: "Is our worship fit for God?" Worship is weekly practice at not being God, and offers the soundtrack for the rest of life. In Romans, we learn that spiritual worship is voluntary self-sacrifice and service to one another and to others in the world. Worship and service go together.

Adults have the capacity to hold this simple act of service alongside the profound reorientation of this question and these statements. Just as children internalize the experience and rhythm of the Feast, our adult participants can engage and expand its profound and parabolic nature. Without words, a great "Aha!" moment may come in this little offering at the end of each lesson, and Sunday morning worship may never be the same. The Feast is a time to offer our prayers, silently or aloud—words forming around the experience of being opened through stories, wondering, and our work. We express our offerings of the heart, and then we share an offering that delights the senses. Taste and see that the Lord is good.

For Course I students, the Feast will also be the time to select a special bead reflecting the story or stories of the day. In a kind of reverse offering, a small bowl is passed and a bead selected by each

---

[26] Capon, *Supper of the Lamb*, 25.

participant. In our last lesson, these beads will be strung, creating a Godly Play® rosary, a meditation tool to remember the stories after our time together has ended. In Courses I and III, the Feast can be festal rather than ferial.

The Dismissal

Saying goodbye is as important as being greeted. Each one is sent out with a blessing. How that might emerge is left to the leadership and the community being formed. Be creative.

Lesson Planning

The brain is not a mechanical object: it is an organic entity. The mind is not a calculator: it is a dynamic process of consciousness. The creative process is not a single ability that lives in one or other region of the body. It thrives on the dynamism between different ways of thinking and being.[27]

Our approach to formation takes this quote to heart. We prepare the whole person for entry into a new way of living, a different way of being in community. As adults in this culture, we have been taught to think about learning as a didactic process of receiving small sequential chunks of information delivered by direct instruction. We analyze, compartmentalize, organize, memorize, and process content and data. Competition drives success and failure. And we *are* driven.

What follows is an array of reflections and ideas to enrich the experience of learning in a more generous way, especially for those in preparation for baptism, confirmation, reception, and reaffirmation of vows. We will be steeped in story and experience, listening to each other, sitting quietly and allowing the amazing consciousness that sets us apart from the rest of Creation, allowing this consciousness to fashion each one into the wondrous and unique human being that God calls beloved. We will not be driven but instead, we will be carried along in the river of life through the waters of baptism.

These lesson plans are designed for all four courses and are simply a guide. My hope is that you will be as creative and flexible as your particular situation allows. *The Complete Guide* is your primary resource and provides the foundation. These lesson plans are meant to guide your process without restricting your creativity. Together we will learn. Each lesson provides an overview, with suggestions for how to move through the time provided. In addition to including the Godly Play® stories, these lesson plans provide additional ideas and resources to adjust to the particular needs of our adult participants. The lesson

---

[27] Robinson, *Out of Our Minds*, 121.

plans will indicate when something unique to that lesson (or course) needs to be done. Your key resource is found in *The Complete Guide*, your primary and critical resource for all things Godly Play®.

I cannot overstate the importance of being trained and well versed in the content of *The Complete Guide*. The content in Volume 1 provides an excellent review of the history, method, and materials that will prepare you for this work. *Teaching Godly Play* is also an excellent primer, and *Children and the Theologians* (Chapter 9 in particular) provides a fascinating theological review of our understanding of the place of the child in church history.[28] Finally, *The Spiritual Guidance of Children* tells the larger story of Godly Play® and its development.

We are just beginning to explore how to use Godly Play® with adults, so now is the time to be creative and inventive. I hope you will let your own creativity enter into this new way. As we play and share experiences of what works best, we will all be blessed. Jerome Berryman says there are three kinds of knowing:

- Knowing of the body through the senses using physical artifacts
- Knowing of the spirit by contemplation
- Knowing of the mind by reason

The spiritual practice that is Godly Play® is all about becoming human. In a world where children are being turned into weapons, our most important work may be helping children become human. We, too, aspire to rediscover our own humanity in the presence of our loving God, a new and more integrated way of knowing.

Lesson Plan Outline

Lesson Overview

- A short review of the story to be used, including the genre.
- Remember: Everything you need for the story and the method is available in *The Complete Guide*.

---

[28] Berryman, *Children and Theologians*, Chapter 9.

Notes for Storytellers

- Special notes to help the Storyteller get ready. This will vary, depending on which course is being used.

Getting Ready

- Remember to help the circle get ready. It can be more difficult with adults than children. Many arrive distracted, anxious, and weary. Just breathe.

Telling the Story

- Practicing the story many times is a joy.
- Remember *The Complete Guide* contains everything you need, and *YouTube Godly Play* is very helpful as you practice.
- When the story is in you and when you can tell it through your hands, heart, and voice—your whole body—then you are ready.

The Wondering

- Augustine said: "People travel to wonder at the height of mountains, at the huge waves of the sea, at the long courses of rivers, at the vast compass of the ocean, at the circular motions of the stars: and they pass by themselves without wondering."
- To paraphrase Berryman, wondering in Godly Play® is key to inhabiting a language, not just telling stories. Each story provides the wondering options as participants encounter the Holy One.
- As you prepare, your own wondering may be insightful. Remember silence is a gift—allowing space for silence in the time of wondering is sometimes hard for the Storyteller, especially when working with adults. Just breathe.

Role Play (for Course II)

- *Teaching Godly Play* is a great resource to help adults learn a new way of working with children. Parents and grandparents will find new ways to be present to their children and grandchildren and, using role play, can begin to practice this open and nonevaluative way of being with children.

The *Work*

- Liberating adults for their work is a challenge. We are so oriented around productivity that it is hard to simply express what we are feeling through our senses.

- Course I members will each have a container filled with materials—it is for them. Their work does not have to be shared, examined, or exhibited, and they will also create an Object Box (*The Complete Guide to Godly Play*, Volume 1, pp. 22–24) and meditation beads to support their ongoing spiritual practice. The Object Box stories will be told during the work time from Lesson 6 through Lesson 10. Two or three stories can be told each lesson day.

- Other groups will have a shorter period for their work/ response but may be encouraged to continue to engage even after the lesson has ended.

- Be creative in your preparation for this part of the course.

Table Time (for Course I)

In our work with adults, we will engage in a bit of direct, explicit, and systematic instruction of intentional knowledge that allows for a little time to unpack the experience of the story, wondering, and work/ response, acknowledging that we are engaged with adults who may be more facile in moving from experience to the executive center of the brain and processing those experiences at a more conscious level. This is a reversal of our more typical way of presenting small sequential chunks of information (direct instruction) and then discussing it. The opposite approach is one of indirect instruction that invites participants into an experience with no guidance at all. Adults are often frustrated on both counts: direct instruction lacks emotional content, and indirect instruction feels amorphous and vague. Godly Play® represents a third way of learning, beautifully represented in

The Importance of Being Little by Erika Christakis. Teaching is intentional but flexible. It seeds the process and helps the child in all of us flourish.

- The transition from the circle to the tables can be eased with a poem, psalm, hymn, or piece of art (schematic symbols)—something thematically relevant to the lesson but still open ended. Suggestions will be offered, but feel free to choose from your own favorite works of literature, art, or poetry. Poetry can aide in the transition from the work/response to the table and then back into the circle for the Feast.

- After the storytelling, wondering, and response, which move us in and out of the limbic and nonverbal areas of the brain, table time allows what neurobiologists call a "left shift."

We enter the domain of language and analytic thinking. For many of us, this is our comfort zone. Our challenge is to become integrated, left/right, limbic/executive center, head/heart, and mind/body.

- This time can be spent with a short teaching on theological language, perspective on worldview or a bit of history. A bibliography and list of suggested authors are found at the end of the book, and they include some of the author's sources.

- As we finish at the table, we begin to "shift right," leaving the table for the circle and the Feast where we will hold all we have experienced in this gathering. Like poetry, art and photography can also be sources of inspiration. The internet is filled with downloadable art and photographs that can serve as a bridge from the circle to the table and back again into the circle.

The Feast

- Provision for a sharing of prayers and the small Feast will vary from course to course.

- In Course I, participants provide provisions for the Feast beginning in Lesson 3.

- Course I will also include a small bowl holding beautiful beads that will be passed around after the prayers, a reverse offering of sorts. Each participant will select a bead that represents the story of the day. The beads will be strung together on the last lesson, creating a rosary of stories.

The Dismissal

- The sending out will take its own shape depending on the setting.

- Remember this is a time of blessing each participant, a very holy moment to be savored until we gather again.

Remember as you begin, each lesson plan will indicate when something unique to the lessons needs to noted or done. Most lessons are to be followed as described in *The Complete Guide* and if no further instructions are needed in a given section of the lesson plan, then simply follow the instructions in *The Complete Guide*. Remember, we are learning as we go and after a few lessons, each group will begin to take on its own rhythm.

Overview of the Stories

SS = *Sacred Story*
LA = *Liturgical Action*
PA = *Parable*
EN = Enrichment Lesson (all others are core lessons)

Lesson	Story	Reflection
1	The Circle of the Church Year (LA) Volume 2	We begin with an orientation in time and encounter the unique nature of religious language as opposed to all the other languages of our culture—scientific, legal, economic, psychological, socio-logical, political, ethical, philosophical, technological, and even the language of the marketplace. We discover the realm of a different kind of time, the rhythm of beginnings and endings punctuated by an encounter with mystery—the elusive and hidden Holy One.
2	Creation (SS) Volume 2	As infants, we first orient in space and time, and in scripture, we also orient in space and time. We begin with creation out of nothing: first, light—the impulse of energy, wave, and particle. The beauty of beginning at the beginning allows for a graceful emptiness. We start with nothing, but soon we find ourselves sur-rounded by wonder. With these two lessons we are now ready, we are oriented in space and time. Now it is time to get moving: who are we, and where are we going?
3	The Great Family (SS) Volume 2	The desert is a dangerous place, but this story takes us into the desert because being deprived of familiar comforts is often a key to coming to new insights. This story takes us on a journey that will test our willingness to leave what is known. We are stripped down until we reach the time and place where God can come close.
4	The Exodus (SS) Volume 2	The People of God, this Great Family finds itself in a time and place of danger—they are slaves to power and seem helpless to seek a new way. Will freedom come? Are we prepared for the cost and the promise of freedom?
5	The Exile and the Return (SS) Volume 2	We return to the desert and another long journey. It seems that breaking the patterns that lead us into bondage is not easy. Now we prepare to face the truth of our lives. We are ready to share our own stories.

Lesson	Story	Reflection
6	The Holy Family (LA/EN) Volume 3	In this lesson we move from *Sacred Stories* to our own stories. The bridge between the *Sacred Stories* and our stories is the holy family. It is the matrix, the womb out of which new life comes. Using an Object Box we will enter into a new kind of sacred space and time as we begin to share our own stories.
7	Advent and Christmas (LA) Volume 3	From *Sacred Stories* that helped shape identity, we now begin the journey that changes everything. It takes four weeks to get ready to enter into the Mystery of Christmas. Currently the language and the experience are captive to a culture of consumption and transaction. Our work is harder because we feel as if we know this story, but the story we know is nostalgic and trite, wrapped up in a bow, but not in mystery. Recovering meaning and mystery will be the task for these next six weeks.
8	Parable of the Good Shepherd (PA) Volume 3	The gift of parables is another way the elusive God comes to us. These weeks open us to the person of Jesus but often in an oblique way. Robert Capon writes about this as the left-handed power of God.[29] Now wondering becomes our new work.
9	The Faces of Easter (LA) Volume 4	Telling the story this way seems so simple, but where it ends is back at the beginning, the re-creation of the universe. This lesson calls for a great deal of silence.
10	Knowing Jesus in a New Way (LA) Volume 8	Eastertide unfolds in doubt and confusion and then in joy and wonder. The transformation of the disciples calls us to look in the mirror. Are we ready?
11	The Greatest Parable (SS) Volume 8	"The goal of this presentation is to allow the inexhaustible meaning and linguistic complexity of Jesus to shine through with a kind of deep simplicity that it is open to all of us."[30]
12	Baptism (LA) Volume 3 Good Shepherd and World Communion Volume 4	We end here but, as we learned in our lesson on time, in our beginnings are our endings and in our endings are our beginnings. And wonder of wonders, the Feast is on behalf of everyone, in all times and places!

---

[29] Capon, *Parables of the Kingdom*, 27.
[30] Berryman, *The Complete Guide to Godly Play*, Vol. 8, 33.

Course I:

The Heavenly Banquet (Preparation for Baptism, Confirmation, and Reaffirmation of Vows)

This course is the most extensive of the four, involving twelve weekly lessons of ninety minutes each.

The ideal class size is ten to fifteen and is best conducted in a space that is large enough to include a circle (with chairs or cushions) comfortably accommodating fifteen adults, plus tables and chairs for additional conversation and work. Ideally, this course takes place in anticipation of The Great Vigil of Easter, where adults being prepared for baptism will be welcomed into the Church. The themes of *sacred time and space*, *identity*, and *belonging* are a critical part of formation, and we will explore those larger theological categories and themes of *faith, captivity, and freedom, sin and restoration, incarnation, offering, resurrection, transformation, mystery,* and *grace* that play out in the stories as we build the foundational language and establish the rhythmic patterns of gathering, listening, reflecting, responding, Feasting, and being sent out.

Because we are not approaching formation in the more typical classroom setting, creating a safe space for these participants is critical. In the first lesson, we begin at tables to meet and greet each other, share an overview of the series and the materials, review the history of Godly Play®, and talk about the essentials—especially getting ready, the wondering, and the work. We will take our time, creating a safe environment before we go to the storytelling circle to tell/hear the first story.

Desired Outcome

The experience of belonging to the group (being known and valued) and encountering the astonishing story of the Christian people is at the heart of our work. Fluency in our language of faith is a lifelong process, but it begins here. At the end of our twelve lessons, participants will remember the experience of the stories, having engaged "the creative process in action"[31] (flow, play, love, and contemplation), gaining insight into how the language of the Christian people flows out of the heart of Jesus and into their lives. Through that experience they will be able to tell their own stories using symbolic images and action. They will also acquire a working vocabulary of scripture, theology, and liturgy, and begin to use the more abstract theological language with confidence and understanding. They will leave with a deep awareness of their value as a beloved child of God.

Goals of the Storyteller and Participants

- *Gather:* to build a "good circle."
- *Listen and Tell:* to use the Godly Play® stories to expand capacity for wondering, reflection, and silence.
- *Respond:* to recover the creative child within, rediscovering gifts and passions through the work.
- *Celebrate*: to create an environment that allows the class to experience graceful living in the Feast.
- *Depart:* to take the practice of astonishment, wonder, and offering into the world.
- *Teach and Learn:* to learn basic fundamentals of faith through scripture, history, theology, and liturgy.

Schedule

The normal schedule for most ninety-minute lessons is as follows (see each lesson for exceptions):

- *Story:* thirty minutes (including the Wondering)
- *Work:* twenty minutes

---

[31] Berryman, *The Spiritual Guidance of Children*, Preface, x.

- *Study*: twenty minutes (the introductions to the stories from *The Complete Guide* offer useful material for this study of basic theological themes)

- *Feast*: twenty minutes (including prayers and departure)

Room, Materials, and Resources

Space

For Course I, we do not use the Godly Play® space. That space is for the children, intentionally designed for access to materials, containing tables and chairs just the right size—ready for them in every way. The space is both open and boundaried. To help adults enter into the wonder of Godly Play®, we must make clear that becoming like children is not the same thing as pretending to be children. We will take a little more time helping the adults get ready, building a space just for them. The series honors where they are, taking into account that they bring their own stories and experiences with them. Some have been damaged by other experiences, some are anxious about taking this step, and all are on a journey that will create a safe place to belong.

You need a large conference space that allows for a circle accommodating ten to fifteen adults and a table setup in a square for face-to-face conversation. The tables also provide workspace after the storytelling. The space should be as open and uncluttered as possible and must be relatively quiet and light filled. Some participants may need to sit in chairs for the storytelling, and some will prefer the floor. There is no right way, just the way that makes engagement easier. We will move between the circle and the square, learning to shift our focus between more active (direct instruction) learning and the contemplative pace of Godly Play®. Modeling this pattern and encouraging participants to establish this rhythm in the day to day are parts of creating an integrated life; learning how to become centered *and* engaged is our true work.

A small bookcase or open shelving is placed behind the Storyteller, as in a Godly Play® space, providing a focal point. The story of the holy family is placed there at the first gathering and through the following weeks, each new story is available for review and reflection. By the end of the twelve lessons, all the stories are on display, including participants' own Object Boxes, reminding them of the journey they have taken.

Materials and Resources

Because it is likely that the space in which you meet is being used by others, it is helpful to provide each participant with a container to hold the materials—papers and other objects—accumulated during the twelve weeks, which will provide them with a sense of ownership of their work. It should be big enough to hold a three-ring binder, a composition journal, some good art paper, some precut cardstock, colored pens, a good pen or pencil, and other materials as desired. The room should also have available colored drawing pens, paints, clay, scissors, glue, origami papers, colored beads, card stock, fabric, and copies of beautiful photographs and images of nature, spaces, light/darkness, and people.

Two special projects are included in Course 1: an Object Box story of one's life and meditation beads. (See images in the appendix.) During this series, participants will create Object Boxes in order to tell their own stories. They may supply their own special box or use one provided by the leader. Instructions are available on pages 22–24 in *The Complete Guide to Godly Play, Volume 1*. The meditation object includes beads that represent the stories, providing a mnemonic device to help sustain the practice after the course is concluded.

A variety of poetry books, prayer books, hymnals, and Bibles are helpful—and participants can be encouraged to bring their own favorites. The list is not exhaustive. Be creative in providing materials for their work that make sense for adults. Invite the participants to bring food and drink for the Feast after the first two lessons, offering one another the chance to practice the value of a bite of one delicious thing.

Lesson 1: Circle of the Church Year

(*The Complete Guide to Godly Play*, Vol. 2, 23–33)

Lesson Overview

This story is part of the genre we label *Liturgical Action* and is a *Core Presentation*. We begin with an orientation in time and encounter

the unique nature of religious language as opposed to all the other languages of our culture—scientific, legal, economic, psychological, sociological, political, ethical, philosophical, technological, and even the language of the marketplace. We discover the realm of a different kind of time: the rhythm of beginnings and endings, punctuated by an encounter with mystery—the elusive and hidden Holy One. Help participants prepare for this encounter.

Notes for Storytellers

Because this is your first time together, allow time for introductions and an explanation of the course. It is important to spend a few minutes describing the sequence of events for each class. Invite each person to briefly introduce themselves. Describe the desired outcomes for the course and the class agenda. A short overview about the Godly Play® history and method, the lessons, getting ready, wondering, and other useful information found in this text or in *The Complete Guide* will help them prepare.

We begin at the tables so that participants can get oriented to the time and space that will become a nest of sorts. Most adults know how to sit and listen in an auditorium, or classroom with tables, desks, and a podium. Here we have two spaces. The circle is the place where we enter into the story. After we are done with the story and our work, we will convene at the table, crossing a threshold to a different kind of learning. We will then return to the circle for the Feast and dismissal.

Getting Ready

In Godly Play®, children are encouraged to ready themselves; adults, however, may need a little more help. When all participants have gathered, the Storyteller can invite everyone to get in a comfortable position, either in a chair or on the floor, and to close their eyes. For a minute or two, all are invited to breathe deeply, in and out. Breathing deeply brings oxygen into the body, lowering anxiety, releasing the tension we hold in our bodies all the way down to each cell. It also helps participants shift into a different kind of learning mode. Throughout this series of lessons, we will follow a similar pattern of getting ready for our story.

Allow two full minutes for this opening meditation, inviting everyone to sit comfortably, close their eyes, and place their right hand over their heart. Ring the bell or sound the bowl to begin. Breathing in and out through the nostrils, count softly: Breathe in 1,2,3,1 and breathe out 1,2,3,2, breathe in 1,2,3,3, breathe out 1,2,3,4 and breathe in 1,2,3,1 and breathe out 1,2,3,2, breathe in 1,2,3,3 and breathe out 1,2,3,4. Keep the breath going, reminding them that when the mind starts wandering to just come back to the breath.

After two minutes, ring the bell or sound the bowl, signaling the end of the meditation. Listen to the sound until it can no longer be heard. Now we are ready.

Telling the Story of the Circle of the Church Year

Our first lesson is also Lesson 1 in *The Complete Guide*, Volume 2, and begins on page 23.

The Wondering

The Wondering questions are found on page 32 (p. 10 in the digital version of The Circle of the Church Year). At first, the Wondering will be awkward. Adults often think there must be a correct answer or perhaps there is a trick to wondering. Silence can be unbearable. The Storyteller must breathe and let the silence continue until someone is brave enough to respond. The good news is that they will get better and better at Wondering.

The Work

In this first lesson, some of our regular available time for Work was used in the orientation.

The participants will have a chance to look at their containers and the additional art and response resources in the room. (A sample list of items can be found in the appendix.) Even their container should be beautiful and well made. The idea that they are beginning a journey and will accumulate their work will begin to create a sense of value, including what we create and treasure: their container, responses, the rosary, and their own story kept in an Object Box all signal that this is going to be a different kind of learning.

Note: Table Time will sometimes follow the Work for Course I participants.

The Feast

Leaders provide the Feast for the first two lessons, and then class members bring something special for the next nine lessons. (Prepare a sign-up sheet for Lesson 2.) The last lesson may include the Eucharist.

Participants return to the circle for the Feast. After the prayers, they will begin a small project, selecting a bead that represents this first story. Each bead will be chosen with intention as a sign of the mystery in their life. A small bowl will be passed around and each one will select a bead that best represents our story on Time. The bead is the first piece of a tool for meditation that we will assemble over the next twelve weeks. A bead will be selected at each lesson and will provide a *mnemonic tool* for each participant. "A mnemonic device (derived from the ancient Greek word for remembrance) is any learning technique that aids information retention, especially in visual or kinesthetic forms."[32]

In the Godly Play® classroom, the children are immersed into the experience of the space and the spiral curriculum. As we work with adults in a more restrictive and limited environment and time frame, it is useful to reinforce the experience by activating the "medial temporal lobe and hippocampus in which the episodic memory is synthesized."[33] Mnemonic devices are especially useful in helping adults stay connected to the artful stories and experiences of the circle.

The Dismissal

In this holy time each person will be sent off with a blessing from the Storyteller. See *The Complete Guide to Godly Play*, Volume 1, page 58 for thoughts about sending out into the world. The Storyteller can say something such as, "It was wonderful to have you here today."[34]

---

[32] Liddell and Scott, *A Greek-English Lexicon, on Perseus*.

[33] Reagh, et al. Spatial discrimination deficits as a function of mnemonic interference in aged adults with and without memory impairment.

[34] Berryman, *The Complete Guide to Godly Play*, Vol. 1, 58.

Lesson 2: Creation

(*The Complete Guide to Godly Play,* Vol. 2, 41–48)

Lesson Overview

As infants, we first orient in space and time. In scripture, we also orient in space and time. We begin with creation, out of nothing, first light, the impulse of energy—wave and particle. The beauty of beginning at the beginning allows for a graceful emptiness: we begin with nothing, and soon we find ourselves surrounded by wonder. With these first two lessons (Circle of the Church Year and Creation), we are now ready; oriented in space and time, now it is time to get moving. Who are we and where are we going?

Notes for Storytellers

In the beginning, God created the heavens and earth . . .

It is like this in the human realm as well—from nothing but love, a child is born.

We begin our second lesson with the story of Creation, gathering the community into the circle for the second time. This is a *Sacred Story* and one of the *Core Presentations* in Godly Play®. (Remember the four genres include *Sacred Stories, Liturgical Action, Parables,* and *Silence.*)

Jerome Berryman reminds us: "With this lesson we begin to trace the elusive presence of the mystery of God in the story of God's People. We begin to play hide-and-seek with the Holy One and ask, 'What can we know of the Giver by the gift?'"[35]

Developmentally, a child journeys across a threshold called object permanence somewhere between one and two years. This milestone represents the ability to hold an object in one's mind, even when it is not in sight, or present through the other senses. This is the moment when games like "peekaboo" bring delight to child and parents alike;

---

[35] Berryman, *The Complete Guide to Godly Play,* Vol. 2, p. 41; p. 1 in the digital version of Creation.

a special kind of play begins with this ability. It is interesting to note that although this ability is critical to the development of the frontal cortex, its value is often lost in the rational adult who says, "Seeing is believing." We have forgotten how to play.

We discover with the Creation story an opportunity to recover the delight of playing with a Creator who is hidden from view, yet present in the very creation that surrounds us. Our work with adults must rediscover what is key to the Christian life: God fills all of Creation, even when not apparently visible. Young children have far less trouble playing hide-and-seek in the time of wondering than adults. So we will begin with remembering what we cannot see or prove, anchoring ourselves in space and the wonder of creation.

Getting Ready

Remember to slow down and breathe deeply first.

When everyone is quiet and the Storyteller feels the rhythm of the room settling, it is time to begin. After the first few lessons, the Storyteller will begin to get a feel for the group. Some will come in ready to gather for the presentation of the story, and others will bring a world of concerns and anxiety with them. Help the participants get ready by providing a few moments of centering themselves.

Telling the Story of Creation

Remember to be fully prepared, having practiced the story and the questions for wondering. The Creation Story is found in *The Complete Guide to Godly Play*, Volume 2, on pages 41–48.

The Wondering

Again, allow for the silences.

The Work

Shift the community from wondering to their work. With the children, the Storyteller invites each to leave the circle for their work, thus acknowledging that each is valued in the circle. We provide that same invitation to our adult participants. Crossing the threshold and entering into the sacred space of the circle helps set the tone for the experience. Helping each one to begin their response by inviting them to leave the circle allows for a quiet transition. Once the participants have engaged in their response to the story, the Storyteller and Doorperson are there for encouragement. See *The Complete Guide to Godly Play*, Volume 1, pages 53–58 for an overview.

Table Time

Participants gather at the table for conversation about the theological themes. It helps to offer a thematic piece of poetry to reconvene the community. Some suggestions are found in the bibliography, but this is an opportunity to be creative. As the class begins to gel, there may be a poet, musician, or artist who would like to share their own work. In these early lessons of Course I, the table work can be very rewarding. If you have a favorite resource or study guide, allow your own wisdom to guide you in the choice of theological themes and categories. This list is neither definitive nor exhaustive.

Theological Themes and Categories

- Nature of God, Creator
- Light, Darkness, Water, and Earth
- Nature of humanity
- Sabbath
- Time: *Chronos* and *Kairos*

The Feast

The Storyteller and Doorperson will serve as hosts for the first two lessons, modeling the hospitality of the servant's heart and offering the invitation to experience community through prayers and the Feast. After the prayers, a small bowl is passed among the participants, each one taking a bead that best represents Creation.

The Dismissal

And always, provide a graceful sending forth.

Lesson 3: The Great Family

(*The Complete Guide to Godly Play*, Vol. 2, 57–64)

Lesson Overview

As adults, we already know the desert is a dangerous place. We also think we know who we are. This story takes us on a journey that will test our willingness to leave what is familiar and comfortable. If Parker Palmer is right about the value in being disillusioned so that we might be stripped of our illusions, this is where it begins. We are stripped down until we reach the time and place where God can come close. This lesson is a *Sacred Story* and one of the *Core Presentations*.

Notes for Storytellers

I have always been amazed at how much adults like the desert box. Just like the children, they want to put their hands into the sand. The story is a very powerful. Don't rush, be mindful of transitions, and set a pace that is marked by deliberate movement, intentional reflection, and the occasional surprise of fresh insight.

Getting Ready

As always, take time to settle and breathe. By now, participants will look forward to this time with anticipation, not anxiety.

Telling the Story of the Great Family

The Complete Guide to Godly Play, Volume 2, page 57 provides background information and additional notes (p. 1 in the digital version of The Great Family). Always take your time with the preparation.

The Wondering

Wondering questions are on page 64 (p. 8 in the digital version of The Great Family). Let your own wondering and preparation expand the possibilities.

The Work

Remind participants that the stories are theirs to work with if they want to get their hands in the sand. Of course, there are also the options of writing, working with art materials, or simply sitting in quiet reflection.

Table Time

Shifting from our Work to the table requires crossing another threshold and presents an opportunity to share a piece of poetry or hymn text to move from silence back into conversation. The first three stories have set the context of time, space, and now identity. We have an opportunity to consider the nature of worldview and culture. The teaching time is short and should be reinforcing the experience of the story, the Wondering, and their Work.

Theological Themes and Categories to Consider

- Worldview

- Identity

- Faith

- Nature of God

- Sacred Space

- Call

After the table time today, instruct participants to prepare their own Object Box stories (see *The Complete Guide*, Volume 1, page 21–23 for ideas; 21–23 in the digital download *How to Lead Godly Play Lessons*). The Storyteller or Doorperson will model this form by sharing their Object Box. These stories should be contained in a small box or basket of participants' choosing, selecting no more than seven objects and an underlay. The stories should be no more than five minutes in length and will begin to be presented after the story of the holy family in Lesson 6. We will do a few each lesson, between Lesson 6 and Lesson 9, until all are done.

The Feast

This will be the first Feast hosted by two members of the class.

After the prayers, a small bowl is passed among the participants, each one taking two beads that best represents Abram and Sarai.

The Dismissal

Lesson 4: The Exodus

(*The Complete Guide to Godly Play*, Vol. 2, 65–72)

Lesson Overview

The People of God, this Great Family, found itself in a time and place of danger—they were slaves to power and seemed helpless to seek a new way. Would freedom come? Are we prepared for the cost and the promise of freedom? This is a *Sacred Story* and part of the *Core Presentations*.

Notes for Storytellers

"God was with the People as they went out (the literal meaning of the word *exodus*) from slavery into freedom through the water. The People of God have looked back to this time to sustain them when God is hidden and they feel lost. For Christians, Baptism reawakens this event, especially when commemorated in the Easter Vigil. . . . In these stories, we continue to evoke the People's experiences of God's elusive presence."[36]

Getting Ready

The class should be shifting into the posture of preparing automatically, but it always helps to stop and breathe.

Telling the Story of the Exodus

The Story of the Exodus begins on page 65 of Volume 2 of *The Complete Guide to Godly Play*.

The Wondering

The Wondering questions are on pages 71–72 (7–8 in the digital version of The Exodus), concluding with a taste of unleavened bread.

The Work

The great themes of captivity and freedom provide a rich opportunity for work to be done. Participants are already working on their own stories, and these themes may be especially important to some of

---

[36] Berryman, *The Complete Guide to Godly Play*, Vol. 2, p. 65; p. 1 in the digital version of The Exodus.

them. Remember we are tapping into more hidden aspects of our lives; sometimes, this work evokes significant experiences from one's past.

Table Time

Consider transitioning participants from their Work to Table Time with a great piece of poetry that reflects the themes of this lesson and invites responses. John O'Donohue, *To Bless the Space Between Us,* "For a New Beginning" is a wonderful poem as we begin this conversation). You could ask, for example: What word or phrase from this poem jumps out at you?

Theological Themes and Categories

- Slavery and Freedom

The Feast

Participants provide the Feast.

After the prayers, pass the small bowl of beads among the participants, each one taking two for the Exodus.

The Dismissal

Lesson 5: The Exile and the Return

(*The Complete Guide to Godly Play*, Vol. 2, 93–99)

Lesson Overview

"Abraham and Sarah traveled away from their home, a land where people thought that gods were in each thing—such as in the sky, in a river, or in a tree. The understanding that 'all of God might be everywhere' sustained Abraham and Sarah as they finally made their way to Canaan, where Isaac was born. And God was there.

"In this lesson, nearly the same arcing journey is taken by God's people, but this time in the opposite direction. And once again, they discover the same truth—God's presence is not here or there but everywhere, waiting. To be found. To find us."[37]

---

[37] Berryman, *The Complete Guide to Godly Play*, Vol. 2, p 93; p. 1 in the digital version of The Exile and the Return.

Notes for Storytellers

We return to the desert and another long journey. Apparently breaking the patterns that lead us into bondage is not easy. For the third week in a row—back to that desert! This is a *Sacred Story* and one of the *Core Presentations*.

In this series for adults, we move quickly through the *Sacred Stories*, leaving many out. One day, if we have been successful in creating an environment where adults experience Godly Play® as spiritual practice, we can move through all the stories. Our goal in this series is to give them enough to create an interior shift and a longing for more.

Now, we prepare to face the truth of our lives. We are getting ready to share our own stories.

Getting Ready

The rhythm is set. Today we return to the desert one final time.

Telling the Story of the Exile and the Return

This story is found on page 93 of Volume 2 of *The Complete Guide*.

The Wondering

The Wondering is found on page 98 of Volume 2 (p. 6 in the digital version of The Exile and the Return).

The Work

Participants continue to work on their own stories.

Table Time

Transition from the Story and their Work with a psalm or passage like Ecclesiastes 3:1–13.

This may be a good time to do a short overview of the Hebrew Scripture (our Old Testament). To this point we have only experienced a few stories and important figures from Hebrew Scripture; next week we move into the Christian story.

Theological Themes and Categories

- Sin and redemption
- Restoration and reinvention

- Prophets
- Captivity and Freedom

The Feast

Participants provide the Feast.

After the prayers, a small bowl is passed among the participants, each one taking two beads that best represents the Exiles.

The Dismissal

Lesson 6: The Holy Family

(*The Complete Guide to Godly Play*, Vol. 3, 20–26)

Lesson Overview

Godly Play® has the potential to shift one from the *existential vacuum* (emptiness) to a place of *existential meaning* (full integration). Jerome Berryman says it this way:

> The holy family is the *matrix*—the Latin word for womb—out of which new life comes. This story is the story of the re-creation of the universe, Christ's incarnation changes everything. . . . The axis of life in the Christian tradition is birth-death-rebirth.[38]

The holy family is the pivot around which the whole system moves.

Notes for Storytellers

This lesson we move from *Sacred Stories* to our own stories. The holy family is an *Enrichment Lesson* and also reflects *Liturgical Action*. For the children, it is repeated each time there is a change of seasons as a reminder of the changing colors and the rhythm of seasons. The holy family sits in the center of the Focal Shelf in the Godly Play® space; "We find existential meaning in our lives, in the places into which we are born, and through the network of these relationships. The 'answer' to life is not a propositional statement or verbal key. Instead of an

---

[38] Berryman, *The Complete Guide to Godly Play*, Vol. 3, p. 20; p. 1 in the digital version of The Holy Family.

answer, we find a 'home,' every day, in the midst of these relationships of love and creating."[39]

This lesson represents for us an opportunity to tell our own stories. During the first few weeks we have anchored ourselves in time and space; we have addressed issues of identity, faith, slavery, freedom, sin and redemption, restoration, and reinvention. Now we are ready to place our own stories alongside those of the people of God. We begin with this pivotal story.

"The birth-death-rebirth axis is perceived through the naming of the holy family, and through the careful, respective moving of the figures. We, like the holy family, are invited to be co-creators in the biological, psychological, social and spiritual spheres of life.[40]

The sequence for this lesson will be different. We will get ready, tell the story, wonder, and then begin to tell our stories.

Getting Ready

Participants may still experience a bit of anxiety today as they get ready to tell their own stories.

(Reminder: When all participants have gathered, the Storyteller can invite everyone to get in a comfortable position, either in a chair or on the floor, and to close their eyes. For a minute or two, all are invited to breathe deeply, in and out. Breathing deeply brings oxygen into the body, lowering anxiety and releasing the tension we hold in our bodies all the way down to each cell. It also helps participants shift into a different kind of learning mode.)

Telling the Story of the Holy Family

The Story is found in the *The Complete Guide*, Volume 3, pages 20–26.

The Wondering

The Wondering is found on page 26 (p. 7 in the digital version of The Holy Family).

---

[39] Berryman, *The Complete Guide to Godly Play*, Vol. 3, p. 20; p. 1 in the digital version of The Holy Family.

[40] Berryman, *The Complete Guide to Godly Play*, Vol. 3, pp. 20–21; pp. 1–2 in the digital version of The Holy Family.

The Work—Object Boxes (Telling Our Stories)

In this lesson, the Work of participants shifts. We will stay in the circle, leaving the story in place. We hear two or three of their stories, each taking between five or six minutes. The use of Object Box stories leads us into a new kind of sacred space and time that can be deeply personal and sometimes intensely felt. Be sensitive to the group and the Storyteller.

Other Courses continue as usual with work/response time.

Table Time

Transitioning to the table provides an opportunity for participants to talk about the experience of sharing their own stories. Reflection questions are found in *The Complete Guide*, Volume 1, page 24. This is a point where the community begins to bond. The Storyteller will then bring the theological themes into the conversation. With our Object Box stories, we are now looking at our own lives and recognizing that the opportunity to be restored (to go back) and to reinvent one's life (to go forward) is remarkable work and often unexplored territory for adults.

Theological Themes and Categories

- Incarnation
- Re-creation, Restoration, Reinvention

The Feast

Participants provide the Feast.

The Dismissal

Lesson 7: Advent and Christmas

(*The Complete Guide to Godly Play*, Vol. 3, 27–51)

Lesson Overview

Having already told the story of the holy family, we are now ready to move toward Bethlehem and arrive at the birth of Jesus and the lighting of the Christ Candle. The "pointing prophets" guide us, along with the holy family, the shepherds, and the Magi.

Jerome Berryman says,

> Religious language gives order to our lives, asking us to find what is new and different in the sameness. Religious language is generative language: it calls us to be who we are really supposed to be, creatures who create. In this lesson we are also trying to enter into mystery. We want to come as close to it as we can.[41]

To enter into mystery, we cannot stand back and analyze or rationalize. Such work is suited more for mathematics and science. As we tell this story, we are also telling our own stories. Remember they are also filled with wonder and mystery.

Notes for Storytellers

From *Sacred Stories* that helped shape identity, we now begin the journey that changes everything. It takes four weeks to get ready to enter into the Mystery of Christmas, but we will take that journey all at once. This is part of our *Liturgical Action* and an *Enrichment Presentation*. Currently the language and the experience of Christmas are captive to a culture of consumption and transaction. Our work is harder because we feel as if we know this story, but the story we know is nostalgic and trite, wrapped up in a bow but not in mystery. Recovering meaning and mystery of the whole Christian story will be the task for these next six weeks.

Getting Ready

Continue to spend a couple of minutes with the breath prayers, helping move everyone into a more receptive and integrated mindset.

Telling the Story of Advent and Christmas

The story is found in the *The Complete Guide*, Volume 3, pages 27–52. Also read "A Children's Liturgy for Christmas," and the *Enrichment Lessons* of the Mystery of Christmas and Epiphany (52–69). We will

---

[41] Berryman, *The Complete Guide to Godly Play*, Vol. 3, p. 35; p. 9 in the digital document Advent Compilation, which contains all of the Advent lessons.

be telling the whole story in this one lesson. It will take a little longer, and, as you are comfortable, you can adapt relevant words and phrases from the *Enrichment Lessons* to the story.

The Wondering

There are no Wondering questions for this story. *Silence* is a most welcome companion to this story.

The Work—Object Boxes

Participants continue to share their stories during the Work time, staying in the circle and leaving their Object Box stories with the Advent and Christmas stories. The Storyteller can shift from the Reflections on the Object Box stories in the circle to the theological themes at the table. After reflections, all the stories can be put away and the group can move to the tables.

Table Time

A good transition can be made with the recitation of the Magnificat found in the Book of Common Prayer, page 65 or 91 or Luke 1:46–55.

Theological Themes and Categories

- Birth
- Incarnation

The Feast

Participants provide the Feast.

After the prayers, pass the small bowl of beads among the participants, each one taking two: the first for Advent and the second for the Great Mystery of Christmas.

The Dismissal

Lesson 8: Parable of the Good Shepherd

(*The Complete Guide to Godly Play*, Vol. 3, 77–86)

Lesson Overview

The primary sheep-and-shepherd parable of Jesus, recognized as authentic by many scholars, tells of the shepherd who searches for the one sheep that is lost and leaves the ninety-nine to do so. In this presentation, the gate is left open as the shepherd searches for the sheep, but you will also find that many of life's conflicts find meaning and resolution in the themes from Psalm 23 and John 10, also present in the lesson.

The term *parable* can have a wide meaning. This lesson is more of an identity statement of Jesus than a parable.

Notes for Storytellers

The gift of parables is another way the elusive God comes to us. These weeks open us to the person of Jesus, but often in an oblique way. Now Wondering becomes our new Work. This is a *parable*, one of the four genres in Godly Play®.

Getting Ready

Telling the Story of the Parable of the Good Shepherd

The Parable of the Good Shepherd is found in *The Complete Guide*, Volume 3, pages 77–86.

The Wondering

The Work—Object Boxes

Participants continue to share their stories and Object Boxes.

Table Time

Transition with Psalm 23.

Theological Themes and Categories

- Mystery
- Parable

The Feast

Participants provide the Feast.

After the prayers, pass the small bowl of beads among the participants, each one taking a bead that best represents the story of the day.

The Dismissal

Lesson 9: The Faces of Easter I–VII

(*The Complete Guide to Godly Play*, Vol. 4, 32–63

Lesson Overview

As we begin this lesson, we note that we prepare for the second great mystery, the Mystery of Easter. Lent is the season of preparation for Easter. The *Faces of Easter I–VII* moves us toward the Mystery by presenting the stories of Christ's journey toward the cross and resurrection. The *Liturgical Action* of the Faces of Easter is a *Core Presentation*. The children spend the six weeks of Lent to hear the whole story. We will move through them all in today's lesson.

Notes for Storytellers

Telling the story this way seems so simple, and yet it ends back at the beginning: the re-creation of the universe. This lesson calls for much silence. *Practice this lesson until you know it well.* You will guide adults through a story they *think* they know, allowing it to flower in unexpected ways. The potential for integrating all they have learned or thought of as separate and disconnected is great.

When done in a Godly Play® space, the children are invited during the Wondering to make these connections with objects in the room.

Enrich the experience by taking your time, inviting silence and encouraging connections to participants' own stories and memories. Today, as Object Box stories continue to be offered during the work

time, staying in the circle will take on an even more significant meaning as the Faces of Easter and the Object Box personal stories offer a sense of connection, a kind of side-by-side view. The flow of this lesson brings a new level of integration as the Story and our stories flow together. The theological themes align the personal and the profound, providing insight and a sense of unity.

Getting Ready

As always, bring your own quiet spirit to the circle.

Telling the Story of the Faces of Easter

The Story begins in *The Complete Guide* in Volume 4 on page 32 and continues through several lessons, ending on page 68.

The Wondering

The Wondering questions are found in Volume 4 of *The Complete Guide* on pages 35, 41, 46, 51, 56, 62 and 68. (In the digital version they are found on pages 4, 10, 15, 20, 25, 31 and 37 of the download titled "The Faces of Easter Compilation").

The Work—Object Boxes

If the Wondering has helped make connections with the whole language, participants' personal stories are also beginning to connect in significant ways. The group will remain in the circle for their own Object Box stories. Leave the *Faces of Easter* in the center of the circle and invite those telling Object Box stories to each offer their own story. When the Object Box stories are done, the Storyteller then facilitates the Reflection on the stories (*The Complete Guide*, Volume 1, 21–24).

From this point on, the group will remain in the circle, integrating the Story, the Object Box stories, and the Theological Themes and Categories.

In the time remaining, the theological themes may help the participants see how their own stories, like the Faces of Easter, are filled with wonder. The Storyteller can then invite everyone to get ready for the Feast, leaving all the Object Boxes (from this lesson) in the circle along with the Faces of Easter.

Theological Themes and Categories

- Birth
- Wisdom
- Baptism
- Healing
- Offering
- Suffering and betrayal
- Resurrection

The Feast

Participants provide the Feast.

After the prayers, pass the small bowl of beads among the participants, each one taking two: the first for the Faces of Easter and the second for the Great Mystery of Easter.

Very likely, from this point on, the time in the circle will become more comfortable than sitting at the tables. As such, each group should develop its own rhythm. It is important for the Storyteller and Doorperson to be mindful of the comfort level of their participants.

The Dismissal

Lesson 10: Knowing Jesus in a New Way

(*The Complete Guide to Godly Play*, Vol. 8, 80–131)

Lesson Overview

"The season of Easter (Eastertide) extends the experience of Easter Sunday for six weeks, but it also helps prepare for the coming of the Mystery of Pentecost. This period is a transition between Jesus' earthly ministry and the coming of the Holy Spirit."[42]

---

[42] Berryman, *The Complete Guide to Godly Play*, Vol. 8, p. 124; p. 1 in the digital version of Knowing Jesus in a New Way, Part 7: Known by the Holy Spirit.

Notes for Storytellers

Eastertide unfolds in doubt and confusion, and it then moves to joy and wonder. The transformation of the disciples calls us to look in the mirror. Are we ready?

This is a big lesson to prepare for, and, like the Faces of Easter, is done over a series of weeks with the children. In church, we hear these stories from the three-year cycle of the Revised Common Lectionary but never experience them in this rhythmic sequence. *Knowing Jesus in a New Way* is a powerful conclusion to the Lent and Easter cycle, culminating with Pentecost. As always, it is important for the Storyteller and Doorperson to be ready.

Getting Ready

As always, we prepare with silence and a few moments of breathing deeply.

Telling the Story of Knowing Jesus in a New Way

This Story is found in *The Complete Guide*, Volume 8 beginning on page 80 and concluding on page 131 and in the digital version as Knowing Jesus in a New Way, Parts 1 to 7.

The Wondering

When done in a Godly Play® space, the children are invited during the wondering to make these connections with objects in the room. If a Godly Play® space is available, this would be a good time to visit the room. If not, in our space, the first nine stories will be in the room. We also have our imaginations and the Wondering can be equally fruitful even if more symbolic or representative.

Taking time, inviting silence, and encouraging connections to their own stories and memories make this experience rich.

The Work—Object Boxes

Continue with the telling of participants' stories, and remain in the circle.

Theological Themes and Categories

- Resurrection
- Salvation
- The Body of Christ

The Feast

Participants provide the Feast.

After the prayers, pass the small bowl of beads among the participants, each one taking two that best represent the story of the day (Knowing Jesus) and the Great Mystery of Pentecost.

The Dismissal

Lesson 11: The Greatest Parable

(*The Complete Guide to Godly Play*, Vol. 8, 32–62)

Lesson Overview

This lesson is the only one that can be presented without words. We will tell it with words, allowing the elusive presence of God to speak to everyone in the circle. The introduction and notes in *The Complete Guide*, Volume 8 are very important. Preparing for this lesson will take time.

Jerome Berryman tells us:

These lessons present Jesus' public ministry and the relation of his presence to the whole Christian language system. This is a parable, because Jesus is not a window through which God can be glimpsed passing by. Rather, Jesus is an embodiment of God in the frailty and finitude of a human being. Like a parable, Jesus' life hides as well as reveals. It hides and reveals both the divinity and humanity of Jesus, but also with grace, and to a lesser degree, the divinity and humanity in our lives as well.

This is "The Greatest Parable" because Jesus is the source of parables. He is the "Parable Maker"; out of whole life comes our *Sacred Stories*, *Liturgical Action*, and *Silence*, as well as *Parables*. This lesson, therefore, needs to draw to itself and express the whole Christian language system as represented in the Godly Play® room.[43]

---

[43] Berryman, *The Complete Guide to Godly Play*, Vol. 8, p. 32; p. 1 in the digital version, titled The Greatest Parable [the Presentation with Words, Part 1].

Notes for Storytellers

The goal of this presentation is to "allow the inexhaustible meaning and linguistic complexity of Jesus to shine through with a kind of deep simplicity that it is open to all of us."[44] If it is possible to use the Godly Play® space for this story, this would be the time to bring participants to the room to experience the whole language system.

We are almost at the ending of our time together, but as we know, we are also on the threshold of a new beginning. The end of this story offers just one Wondering question: *Now, I wonder what goes here. . . .*

Getting Ready

Telling the Story of the Greatest Parable

This story is found in *The Complete Guide*, Volume 8, beginning on page 32.

The Wondering

With just one question and the very contemplative moment that comes at the end of this story, the invitation to make a response in the time set aside for their work provides an opportunity to explore the whole room—to see what fills in the gaps of their experience in this course. Maybe they will want more. By this time, the circle and the tables will have become indistinguishable. We are part of the Great Family.

The Work and the Table Time Merge

A couple of my favorite poems are St. Symeon the New Theologian, "We Awaken in Christ's Body" found in *Mystical Hope* by Cynthia Bourgeault, and "The Second Sorrowful Mystery: Mother Wisdom Speaks" from *Circle of Mysteries: the Women's Rosary Book* by Christin Lore Weber. These two pieces offer the context for this last table gathering. Their meditation beads are almost done—only two more left: the two great sacraments of Baptism and Eucharist. Next week we will speak of the mystery of sacraments as we prepare the group for the final gathering.

---

[44] Berryman, *The Complete Guide to Godly Play,* Vol. 8, p. 33; p. 2 in the digital version, titled The Greatest Parable [the Presentation with Words, Part 1].

Theological Themes and Categories

- Transformation
- Realized eschatology
- Our common life as the Body of Christ

The Feast

This will be the last time the participants will provide the Feast.

After the prayers, pass the small bowl of beads among the participants, each one taking a bead that best represents the story of the day.

The Dismissal

Lesson 12: Baptism, the Good Shepherd, and World Communion

(*The Complete Guide to Godly Play*, Vol. 3, 70–76 and Vol. 4, 91–98)

Lesson Overview

Courses 1 and 3: Both of these stories are part of *Liturgical Action* and are *Core Presentations*. They will each be told and then, at the end, the participants will place their Object Boxes in the circle.

Courses 2 and 4: These groups will only do the Baptism story.

Notes for Storytellers

We end here but, as we learned in our very first lesson on time, in our beginnings are our endings and in our endings are our beginnings. We are a changed people, flowing in the river of life as one body.

These two stories anchor us in our holy and sacramental life.

Getting Ready

As we get ready for this final lesson, the Storyteller will make sure that there is an open space on the opposite side of the circle.

Telling the Story of Baptism

Holy Baptism is found in *The Complete Guide*, Volume 3, pages 70–76. There will be no Wondering with this lesson. The Storyteller will leave this story out and move to the other side of the circle to tell the second story.

Telling the Story of the Good Shepherd and World Communion

The lesson on the Good Shepherd and World Communion is found in Volume 4, pages 91–98.

The Wondering

At the end of the World Communion, the wondering will include bringing all the other stories in our series to the circle. There will be no Table Time, but the Storyteller will begin to gather all these experiences together, guiding the conversation to a close.

Theological Themes and Categories

- Transformation
- Eschatology
- The Body of Christ

The Feast

If this series is the culmination of preparation for the Great Vigil or Baptism (and Confirmation, Renewal, or Reception), the Feast can be one last, small, and intimate moment of Holy Communion, using wonderful bread and great wine.

For Course I: The Feast can simply be a chance to sit in the circle together with these two stories, enjoying the light and the company of saints gathered. During this time, pass the basket of beautiful beads around for the last time and let the participants choose the final two beads representing the two sacraments. They should have one bead for Time, one for Creation, six "People of God" beads representing the *Sacred Stories*, one for Advent, one for the Great Mystery of Christmas, one for Parables, one for the Faces of Easter, one for the Great Mystery of Easter, one for Knowing Jesus in a New Way, one for the

Great Mystery of Pentecost, one for the Greatest Parable, and the final two for Baptism and Communion: eighteen beads in all. The beads can be strung while the Storyteller and Doorperson prepare the Feast. This is your Feast, yours to imagine and create, the offering of this community newly constituted as a small part of the Body of Christ.

The Dismissal

This sending out will be a very holy moment but not the end; it is only the beginning.

Course II:

Dessert Only (Preparation for Families Beginning Godly Play®)

These six one-hour lessons provide an experience and an overview of the Godly Play® method. Meeting in the Godly Play® space offers a depth of insight into the method that will support parents' efforts both at home and in church. In this case, we equip parents (grandparents, godparents) with sufficient information and tools to encourage their children at home, even to create their own sacred space. Research tells us that a child is more likely to stay churched if the family has a regular spiritual practice at home. Godly Play® accommodates this beautifully, and this course creates advocates for the ongoing support of Godly Play®.

This course can be offered several times a year as part of the baptismal preparation for parents, grandparents, and sponsors, and can also be used with families whose children are entering Godly Play® for the first time. It is also a good way to recruit new Storytellers. Meeting in the Godly Play® space helps them to be better prepared to support their children and may also prompt them to support the program through gifts for new stories.

After a short overview of the series in the first lesson, we move into the circle, providing chairs for those who need them. We then tell the story. Allowing participants to experience a story and a time of wondering sets the stage for a different kind of work than in the other courses. We will shift from the experience into a time of discussion and conversation about the nature of Godly Play®, unpacking the development, design, research, and value for their child or children.

Desired Outcome

To provide families with a working understanding of the Godly Play® method so that they are able to participate in their child's spiritual development in a more active way, learning to support children in open, non-evaluative, and empowering ways.

Goals of the Storyteller and Participants

- *Gather:* to build a "good circle," modeling the task of gathering and getting ready.
- *Listen and Tell:* to share the story and join in the wondering.
- *Teach and Learn:* to facilitate the conversation about the Godly Play® method.
- *Coach and Practice:* to create role-play opportunities, learning how to support children with the language of open, nonevaluative and empowering questions and comments.

Schedule

The normal schedule for each sixty-minute lesson is as follows:

- *Story:* twenty-five minutes (including wondering)
- *The Method:* twenty minutes (*The Complete Guide* and *Teaching Godly Play* provide information that will help parents understand Godly Play®.)
- *Roleplay:* fifteen minutes

Room, Materials, and Resources

Space

The six lessons of Course II are told in the Godly Play® space. It is sacred space and, as we enter, it is like walking into the whole Bible. The space is for the children. The shelves are just high enough so that they can reach all the stories. In our adult learning time, we talk about the importance of the space and help participants consider sacred space in their own homes, a holy place for their children to occupy when they want to be quiet, do their work, or wonder.

Provide adults chairs for those who find sitting on the floor difficult.

Materials and Resources

Provide copies of *The Complete Guide* and *Teaching Godly Play* for participants' review. At the end of the six weeks, the two Godly Play® illustrated storybooks (*The Great Family* and *The Good Shepherd*) can be offered as a gift to the participants.

Lesson 1: Circle of the Church Year

(*The Complete Guide to Godly Play*, Vol. 2, 23–33)

Lesson Overview

This story is part of the genre we label *Liturgical Action* and is a *Core Presentation*. We begin with an orientation in time and encounter the unique nature of religious language as opposed to all the other languages of our culture—scientific, legal, economic, psychological, sociological, political, ethical, philosophical, technological, and even the language of the marketplace. We discover the realm of a different kind of time: the rhythm of beginnings and endings, punctuated by an encounter with mystery, and the elusive and hidden Holy One.

In this first class, help participants prepare for this encounter.

Notes for Storytellers

Because this is your first time together, allow time for introductions and an explanation of the course.

Welcome participants into the circle and spend a few minutes describing the sequence of events for each class. Invite each person to introduce himself or herself briefly. Using the format you have chosen (Course II), describe the desired outcomes for the course and the class agenda. A short overview about the Godly Play® history and method, the lessons, getting ready, wondering and other useful information found in this text or in *The Complete Guide* will help them prepare for the first lesson.

Getting Ready

In Godly Play®, children are encouraged to ready themselves; however, adults may need a little more help. When all participants have gathered, the Storyteller can invite everyone to get in a comfortable position, either in a chair or on the floor, and to close their eyes. For a minute or two, all are invited to breathe deeply, in and out. Breathing deeply brings oxygen into the body, lowering anxiety, releasing the tension we hold in our bodies all the way down to each cell. This also helps participants shift into a different kind of learning mode. Throughout this series of lessons, we will follow a similar pattern of getting ready for our story.

Begin with this meditation practice, allowing two full minutes, inviting everyone to sit comfortably, close their eyes and place their right hand over their heart. Ring the bell or sound the bowl to begin. Breathing in and out through the nostrils, count softly: Breathe in 1,2,3,1 and breathe out 1,2,3,2, breathe in 1,2,3,3, breathe out 1,2,3,4 and breathe in 1,2,3,1 and breathe out 1,2,3,2, breathe in 1,2,3,3 and breathe out 1,2,3,4. Keep the breath going, reminding them that when the mind starts wandering to just come back to the breath. At two minutes, ring the bell or sound the bowl, signaling the end of the meditation. Listen to the sound until it can no longer be heard. Now we are ready.

Telling the Story of the Circle of the Church Year

Our first lesson is also Lesson 1 in *The Complete Guide*, Volume 2, and begins on page 23.

The Wondering

The Wondering questions are found on page 32 (p. 10 in the digital version of The Circle of the Church Year). At first the Wondering will be awkward. Adults often think there must be a correct answer or perhaps there is a trick to this wondering. Silence can be unbearable. The Storyteller must breathe and let the silence continue until someone is brave enough to respond. The good news is that they will get better and better at Wondering.

In this first lesson, some of our regular available time for Work has been used in the orientation.

The Work

For Course II: Participants will shift from wondering to learning about the Godly Play® method, and taking time to role-play. *Teaching Godly Play* is a key resource especially for understanding how to respond to a child's work in a nonjudgmental way.

The Feast

We are learning and experiencing Godly Play® so that we might be better able to support a child's spiritual development. The Feast for this class should be done in the way the children experience it, each participant taking their turn in preparing and sharing the Feast.

The Dismissal

This is holy time and each person will be sent off with a blessing from the Storyteller. See *The Complete Guide*, Volume 1, page 58 for thoughts about sending out into the world. The Storyteller can say something such as, "It was wonderful to have you here today."[45]

Lesson 2: The Great Family

(*The Complete Guide to Godly Play*, Vol. 2, 57–64)

Lesson Overview

As adults, we already know the desert is a dangerous place. We also think we know who we are. This story takes us on a journey that will test our willingness to leave what is familiar and comfortable. If Parker Palmer is right about the value in being disillusioned so that we might be stripped of our illusions, this is where it begins. We are stripped down until we reach the time and place where God can come close. This is a *Sacred Story* and one of the *Core Presentations*.

Notes for Storytellers

I have always been amazed at how much adults like the desert box. Just like the children, they want to put their hands into the sand.

---

[45] Berryman, *The Complete Guide to Godly Play*, Vol. 1, 58.

This is a very powerful story. Don't rush, be mindful of transitions and set a pace that is marked by deliberate movement, intentional reflection and the occasional surprise that comes when insight is enacted.

Getting Ready

As always, take time to settle and breathe. By now, participants will look forward to this time with anticipation, not anxiety.

Telling the Story of the Great Family

The Complete Guide, Volume 2, page 57 provides background information and additional notes (page 1 in the digital version of The Great Family). Always take your time with the preparation.

The Wondering

Wondering questions are on page 64 (p. 8 in the digital version of The Great Family). Let your own wondering and preparation expand the possibilities.

The Work

Remind participants that the stories are theirs to work with as well as the other options of writing, working with art materials or simply sitting in quiet reflection. Letting the parents, grandparents, and sponsors enter into the work is helpful. After they have a few minutes to do their work, let them practice making a response to each other. Use nonjudgmental language, observing, and wondering.

The Feast

This experience of taking, blessing, breaking, and giving is a very holy moment. Prepare them to be present to each other and the offering.

The Dismissal

Lesson 3: The Holy Family

(*The Complete Guide to Godly Play*, Vol. 3, 20–26)

Lesson Overview

Godly Play® has the potential to shift one from the *existential vacuum* (emptiness) to a place of *existential meaning* (full integration). Jerome Berryman says it this way:

> "The holy family is the *matrix*—the Latin word for womb—out of which new life comes. This story is the story of the re-creation of the universe, Christ's incarnation changes everything.
> "The axis of life in the Christian tradition is birth-death-rebirth."[46]

The holy family is the pivot around which the whole system moves.

Notes for Storytellers

The Holy Family is an *Enrichment Lesson* and reflects *Liturgical Action*. For the children, it is repeated each time there is a change of seasons. It is a reminder of the changing colors and the rhythm of seasons. The holy family sits in the center of the Focal Shelf in the Godly Play® space; "We find existential meaning in our lives, in the places into which we are born, through the network of these relationships. The 'answer' to life is not a propositional statement or verbal key. Instead of an answer, we find a 'home,' every day, in the midst of these relationships of love and creating."[47]

"The birth-death-rebirth axis is perceived through the naming of the holy family, and through the careful, respective moving of the figures. We, like the holy family, are invited to be co-creators in the biological, psychological, social and spiritual spheres of life."[48]

---

[46] Berryman, *The Complete Guide to Godly Play*, Vol. 3, p. 20; p. 1 in the digital version of The Holy Family.

[47] Berryman, *The Complete Guide to Godly Play*, Vol. 3, p. 20; p. 1 in the digital version of The Holy Family.

[48] Berryman, *The Complete Guide to Godly Play*, Vol. 3, pp. 20–21; pp. 1–2 in the digital version of The Holy Family.

Getting Ready

Reminder: When all participants have gathered, the Storyteller can invite everyone to get in a comfortable position, either in a chair or on the floor, and to close their eyes.

Telling the Story of the Holy Family

The Story is found in the *The Complete Guide*, Volume 3, pages 20–26.

The Wondering

The Wondering is found on page 26 (p. 7 in the digital version of The Holy Family).

The Work

Continue as usual with work/response time and role-play.

The Feast

The week, surprise the participants with something really wonderful, a small special treat and perhaps, something special to drink. Perhaps one of the participants would like to provide the Feast for next week.

The Dismissal

Lesson 4: Parable of the Good Shepherd

(*The Complete Guide to Godly Play*, Vol. 3, 77–86)

Lesson Overview

The primary sheep-and-shepherd parable of Jesus, recognized as authentic by many scholars, tells of the shepherd who searches for the one sheep that is lost and leaves the 99 to do so. In this presentation, the gate is left open as the shepherd searches for the sheep, but you will also find that many of life's conflicts find meaning and resolution in the themes from Psalm 23 and John 10, also present in the lesson.

The term *parable* can have a wide meaning. This lesson is more of an identity statement of Jesus than a parable.

Notes for Storytellers

The gift of parables is another way the elusive God comes to us. These weeks open us to the person of Jesus, but often in an oblique way. Now Wondering becomes our new Work. This is a *Parable*, one of the four genres in Godly Play®.

Getting Ready

Telling the Story of the Parable of the Good Shepherd

The Parable of the Good Shepherd is found in *The Complete Guide*, Volume 3, pages 77–86.

The Wondering

The Work

This would be a wonderful time to tell your own story, using an Object Box. Constructing a coherent narrative is part of becoming a fully integrated human being. Helping families to understand that this is a very important part of growing in grace, and their capacity to tell their own stories is a gift to their children.

The Feast

This offering from the participants would enhance the experience.

The Dismissal

Lesson 5: The Faces of Easter I–VII

(*The Complete Guide to Godly Play*, Vol. 4, 32–63)

Lesson Overview

As we begin this lesson, we note that we prepare for the second great mystery, the Mystery of Easter. Lent is the season of preparation for Easter. The Faces of Easter I–VII moves us toward the Mystery by presenting the stories of Christ's journey toward the cross and resurrection. The *Liturgical Action* of the Faces of Easter is a *Core Presentation*. The children spend the six weeks of Lent to hear the whole story. We will move through them all in today's lesson.

Notes for Storytellers

Telling the story this way seems so simple, and yet it ends back at the beginning, the re-creation of the universe. This lesson calls for much silence. *Practice this lesson until you know it well.* You will guide adults through a story they *think* they know, allowing this story to flower in unexpected ways. The potential for integrating all they have learned or thought of as separate and disconnected is great.

When done in a Godly Play® space, the children are invited during the Wondering to make these connections with objects in the room.

Enrich the experience by taking your time, inviting silence and encouraging connections to participants' own stories and memories.

Getting Ready

As always, bring your own quiet spirit to the circle.

Telling the Story of the Faces of Easter

The Story begins in *The Complete Guide* in Volume 4 on page 32 and continues through several lessons, ending on page 68.

The Wondering

The Wondering questions are found in Volume 4 of *The Complete Guide* on pages 35, 41, 46, 51, 56, 62, and 68. In the digital version they are found on pages 4, 10, 15, 20, 25, 31, and 37 of the download titled The Faces of Easter Compilation).

The Work

Today the story will take most of our time. If you are in the Godly Play® room, it would be very meaningful to share how this whole space contributes to the child's experience making connections with the Faces.

The Feast

Again a participant providing the Feast is a nice touch.

The Dismissal

Lesson 6: Baptism

(*The Complete Guide to Godly Play*, Vol. 3, 70–76)

Lesson Overview

This is a very special story for our group, especially if some are preparing for a child or grandchild to be baptized. It is done with great intention and is one of those stories that the children practice again and again.

Notes for Storytellers

We end here but as we learned in our very first lesson on time, in our beginnings are our endings and in our endings are our beginnings. We are a changed people, flowing in the river of life as one body. This story anchors us in this holy and sacramental life.

Getting Ready

As we get ready for this final lesson, the Storyteller leads us one more time in a meditation that prepares the body and the mind for a time of blessing.

Telling the Story of Baptism

Holy Baptism is found in *The Complete Guide*, Volume 3, pages 70–76. There will be no Wondering with this lesson.

The Feast

If this series is the culmination of preparation for baptism, the Feast can be one last, small and intimate moment of Holy Communion, using wonderful bread and great wine.

This is your Feast, yours to imagine and create, the offering of this community newly constituted as a small part of the Body of Christ. If at all possible, the offering of one of the Godly Play® story books to each family participating, sends them home with a reminder that they, too, are part of the tradition of nurturing their child in the language of the Christian people.

The Dismissal

This sending out will be a very holy moment but not the end, only the beginning.

Course III:

Slow-Cooking (Retreat)

This weekend course provides a leisurely pace for a parish retreat. Six stories told over a period of a day and a half allow plenty of time for work, reflection, silence, and building of community. The Godly Play® course will focus on the themes of time, space, identity, and belonging. These themes can help build deeper and more intentional relationships among participants. A beautiful setting and slower pace provide an opportunity for intergenerational family groups or adults-only groups to take their time. The spiritual leader for this kind of event can plan other activities and allot time for workshops, worship, or silence as needed and desired. This is a very easy way to introduce Godly Play® to adults in a congregation and works well as part of an annual retreat for various groups and leadership teams.

The rhythm of a retreat allows for extended lessons, and if it is done in the context of silence between lessons, it creates a rich experience with the *Sacred Stories, Liturgical Action*, and *Parables*. Each lesson can last from ninety minutes to two hours with wonderful options for response in the work time. A longer retreat of two or three days allows for other activities or contemplative rest. This format can be easily adjusted as needed.

Desired Outcome

The desired outcome is to introduce Godly Play® to adults in a setting that allows for deep engagement with a few stories while building community relationships and acquiring sacred language seen through time, space, identity, mystery, and communion.

Goals of the Storyteller and Participants

- *Gather:* to building a "good circle"
- *Listen and Tell:* to foster trust through wondering and silence

- *Respond:* to liberate creativity with extensive time for work
- *Feasting:* to draw the whole experience to a close through the Feast at the end of the retreat

Schedule
Morning Lessons 1 and 2

• Story and Wondering	twenty-five minutes
• Work	forty-five minutes
• Reconvene for Sharing	twenty minutes
• Break	thirty minutes
• Story and Wondering	twenty-five minutes
• Work	forty-five minutes
• Reconvene	twenty minutes
• Lunch and Break	ninety minutes

Afternoon Lessons 3 and 4

• Story and Wondering	twenty-five minutes
• Work	forty-five minutes
• Reconvene for Sharing	twenty minutes
• Break	thirty minutes
• Story and Wondering	twenty-five minutes
• Work	forty-five minutes
• Reconvene	twenty minutes
• Dinner and Break	sixty minutes

Evening Lesson 5

• Story and Wondering	twenty-five minutes
• Work	thirty minutes
• Reconvene for sharing	twenty-five minutes

Morning Lesson 6

• Story and Wondering	twenty-five minutes
• Work	thirty minutes

- The Feast (Eucharist/Worship)   forty-five minutes
- The Dismissal   five minutes

Room, Materials, and Resources

Space

If in a retreat center, locate a room or an area large enough to accommodate the storytelling circle. The age and ability of the group will determine whether chairs or cushions will be needed. An open and airy room is best, and if it can be set apart throughout the retreat time, that is even better.

Materials and Resources

An open shelf holding the six stories used in Course III is helpful. You also need space for art materials. The work of Course III may involve spaces outside, small settings for reflection and workspace for those who want to respond with art. Art materials similar to those in Course I will be needed. In a retreat setting, this can be loosely structured. The final Feast will be the retreat's official worship and can be set up in the circle or moved to a more formal chapel space. Prayer books or service leaflets may be used, and music can be part of the final gathering. Great bread and wonderful wine will make this final time together a reminder of the importance of appreciating small things.

Lesson 1: Circle of the Church Year

(*The Complete Guide to Godly Play*, Vol. 2, 23–33)

Lesson Overview

This story is part of the genre we label *Liturgical Action* and is a *Core Presentation*. We begin with an orientation in time and encounter the unique nature of religious language as opposed to all the other languages of our culture—scientific, legal, economic, psychological, sociological, political, ethical, philosophical, technological, and even the language of the marketplace—we discover the realm of a different kind of time, the rhythm of beginnings and endings, punctuated by an encounter with mystery, the elusive, and the hidden Holy One.

In this first class, help participants prepare for this encounter.

Notes for Storytellers

Because this is your first time together, allow time for introductions and an explanation of the course. Welcome participants into the circle. Using the format for Course III, describe the desired outcomes for the course and the class agenda. A short overview about the Godly Play® history and method, the lessons, getting ready, wondering, and other useful information found in this text or in *The Complete Guide* will help them prepare for the first lesson.

Getting Ready

In Godly Play®, children are encouraged to ready themselves; however, adults may need a little more help. When all participants have gathered, the Storyteller can invite everyone to get in a comfortable position, either in a chair or on the floor, and to close their eyes. For a minute or two, all are invited to breathe deeply, in and out. Breathing deeply brings oxygen into the body, lowering anxiety, releasing the tension we hold in our bodies all the way down to each cell. This also helps participants shift into a different kind of learning mode. Throughout this series of lessons, we will follow a similar pattern of getting ready for our story.

Begin with this meditation practice, allowing two full minutes, inviting everyone to sit comfortably, close their eyes and place their right hand over their heart. Ring the bell or sound the bowl to begin. Breathing in and out through the nostrils, count softly: Breathe in 1,2,3,1 and breathe out 1,2,3,2, breathe in 1,2,3,3, breathe out 1,2,3,4 and breathe in 1,2,3,1 and breathe out 1,2,3,2, breathe in 1,2,3,3 and breathe out 1,2,3,4. Keep the breath going, reminding them that when the mind starts wandering to just come back to the breath. At two minutes, ring the bell or sound the bowl, signaling the end of the meditation. Listen to the sound until it can no longer be heard. Now we are ready.

Telling the Story of the Circle of the Church Year

Our first lesson is also Lesson 1 in *The Complete Guide*, Volume 2, and begins on page 23.

The Wondering

The Wondering questions are found on page 32 (p. 10 in the digital version of The Circle of the Church Year). At first the Wondering will be awkward. Adults often think there must be a correct answer or perhaps there is a trick to this wondering. Silence can be unbearable. The Storyteller must breathe and let the silence continue until someone is brave enough to respond. The good news is that they will get better and better at Wondering.

In this first lesson, some of our regular available time for Work has been used in the orientation.

Work

With the luxury of time and resources, including the retreat space itself, the response/work time can be extended and many creative materials can enhance this experience. If this is a silent retreat, talking only during the wondering and the time of prayer, reflection, and sharing after the work is an option.

The Feast

Participants reconvene for prayers and sharing work, coming together for the Feast only after the last story.

The Dismissal

This is holy time, and each person will be sent off with a blessing from the Storyteller. See The Complete Guide, Volume 1, page 58 for thoughts about sending out into the world. The Storyteller can say something such as, "It was wonderful to have you here today."[49]

Lesson 2: Creation

(The Complete Guide to Godly Play, Vol. 2, 41–48)

Lesson Overview

As infants, we first orient in space and time. In scripture, we also orient in space and time. We begin with creation, out of nothing, first

---

[49] Berryman, The Complete Guide to Godly Play, Vol. 1, 58.

light, the impulse of energy—wave and particle. The beauty of beginning at the beginning allows for a graceful emptiness—we begin with nothing, but soon we find ourselves surrounded by wonder. With these two lessons, we are now ready; oriented in space and time, now it is time to get moving. Who are we and where are we going?

Notes for Storytellers

In the beginning, God created the heavens and earth. . . .

It is like this in the human realm as well—from nothing but love, a child is born.

We begin our second lesson with the story of Creation, gathering the community into the circle for the second time.

This is a *Sacred Story* and one of the *Core Presentations* in Godly Play®. (Remember the four genres include *Sacred Stories, Liturgical Action, Parables,* and *Silence.*)

Jerome Berryman reminds us: "With this lesson we begin to trace the elusive presence of the mystery of God in the story of God's People. We begin to play hide-and-seek with the Holy One and ask, 'What can we know of the Giver by the gift?' "[50]

Developmentally, a child journeys across a threshold called object permanence, somewhere between one and two years. This milestone represents the ability to hold an object in one's mind, even when it is not in sight (or present through the other senses). This is the moment when games like "peekaboo" bring delight to child and parents alike—a special kind of play begins with this ability. It is interesting to note that although this ability is critical to the development of the frontal cortex, its value is often lost in the rational adult who says, "Seeing is believing." We have forgotten how to play.

We discover with the Creation story an opportunity to recover the delight of playing with a Creator who is hidden from view, yet present in the very creation that surrounds us. Our work with adults must undo and rediscover what is key to the Christian life, God fills

---

[50] Berryman, *The Complete Guide to Godly Play*, Vol. 2, p. 41; p. 1 in the digital version of Creation.

all of Creation, even when not apparently visible. Young children have far less trouble playing hide-and-seek in the time of wondering than adults. So this is where we will start, remembering what we cannot see or prove, anchoring ourselves in space and the wonder of creation.

Getting Ready

Remember to slow down and breathe deeply first.

When everyone is quiet and the Storyteller feels the rhythm of the room settling, it is time to begin. After the first few lessons, the Storyteller will begin to get a feel for the group. Some will come in ready to gather for the presentation of the story, and others will bring a world of concerns and anxiety with them. Help the participants get ready by providing a few moments of centering themselves.

Telling the Story of Creation

Remember to be fully prepared, having practiced the story and the questions for wondering. The Creation Story is found in *The Complete Guide*, Volume 2, on pages 41–48.

The Wondering

Again, allow for the silences.

The Work

It is now time to shift the community from wondering to their work. With the children, the Storyteller invites each to leave the circle for their work, thus acknowledging that each is valued in the circle. We provide that same invitation to our adult participants— crossing the threshold and entering into the sacred space of the circle helps set the tone for the experience. Helping each one to begin their response by inviting them to leave the circle allows for a quiet transition. Once the participants have engaged in their response to the story, the Storyteller and Doorperson are there for encouragement. See *The Complete Guide*, Volume 1, pages 53–58 for an overview.

The Feast

Reconvene after the work time, and offer prayers and reflections on the experience.

The Dismissal

And always, provide a graceful sending forth.

Lesson 3: The Great Family

(*The Complete Guide to Godly Play*, Vol. 2, 57–64)

Lesson Overview

As adults, we already know the desert is a dangerous place. We also think we know who we are. This story takes us on a journey that will test our willingness to leave what is familiar and comfortable. If Parker Palmer is right about the value in being disillusioned so that we might be stripped of our illusions, this is where it begins. We are stripped down until we reach the time and place where God can come close. This is a *Sacred Story* and one of the *Core Presentations*.

Notes for Storytellers

I have always been amazed at how much adults like the desert box. Just like the children, they want to put their hands into the sand. This is a very powerful story. Don't rush, be mindful of transitions, and set a pace that is marked by deliberate movement, intentional reflection, and the occasional surprise that comes when insight is enacted.

Getting Ready

As always, take time to settle and breathe. By now, participants will look forward to this time with anticipation, not anxiety.

Telling the Story of the Great Family

The Complete Guide Volume 2, Lesson 4, page 57 provides background information and additional notes (p. 1 in the digital version of The Great Family). Always take your time with the preparation.

The Wondering

Wondering questions are on page 64 (p. 8 in the digital version of The Great Family). Let your own wondering and preparation expand the possibilities.

The Work

Remind participants that the stories are theirs to work with as well as the other options of writing, working with art materials, or simply sitting in quiet reflection.

The Feast

Gather for prayers and reflections

The Dismissal

Lesson 4: The Holy Family

(*The Complete Guide to Godly Play*, Vol. 3, 20–26)

Lesson Overview

Godly Play® has the potential to shift one from the *existential vacuum* (emptiness) to a place of *existential meaning* (full integration). Jerome Berryman says it this way:

> "The holy family is the *matrix*—the Latin word for womb—out of which new life comes. This story is the story of the re-creation of the universe, Christ's incarnation changes everything.
> "The axis of life in the Christian tradition is birth-death-rebirth."[51]

The holy family is the pivot around which the whole system moves.

Notes for Storytellers

The holy family is an *Enrichment Lesson* and reflects *Liturgical Action*. For the children, it is repeated each time there is a change of seasons. It is a reminder of the changing colors and the rhythm of seasons. The holy family sits in the center of the Focal Shelf in the Godly Play® space; "We find existential meaning in our lives, in the places into which we are born, through the network of these relationships. The 'answer' to life is not a propositional statement or verbal key. Instead

---

[51] Berryman, *The Complete Guide to Godly Play*, Vol. 3, p. 20; p. 1 in the digital version of The Holy Family.

of an answer, we find a 'home,' every day, in the midst of these relationships of love and creating."[52] We begin with this pivotal story. "The birth-death-rebirth axis is perceived through the naming of the holy family, and through the careful, respective moving of the figures. We, like the holy family, are invited to be co-creators in the biological, psychological, social, and spiritual spheres of life."[53]

Getting Ready

Practice two minutes of the breath prayer.

Telling the Story of the Holy Family

The Story is found in the *The Complete Guide*, Volume 3, pages 20–26.

The Wondering

The Wondering is found on page 26 (p. 7 in the digital version of The Holy Family).

The Work

Continue to explore the richness of time and space as part of the retreat experience.

The Feast

Share prayers, reflections, and the work of this story.

The Dismissal

Lesson 5: Parable of the Good Shepherd

(*The Complete Guide to Godly Play*, Vol. 3, 77–86)

Lesson Overview

The primary sheep-and-shepherd parable of Jesus, recognized as authentic by many scholars, tells of the shepherd who searches for the

---

[52] Berryman, *The Complete Guide to Godly Play*, Vol. 3, p. 20; p. 1 in the digital version of The Holy Family.

[53] Berryman, *The Complete Guide to Godly Play*, Vol. 3, pp. 20–21; pp. 1–2 in the digital version of The Holy Family.

one sheep that is lost and leaves the 99 to do so. In this presentation, the gate is left open as the shepherd searches for the sheep, but you will also find that many of life's conflicts find meaning and resolution in the themes from Psalm 23 and John 10, also present in the lesson.

The term *parable* can have a wide meaning. This lesson is more of an identity statement of Jesus than a parable.

Notes for Storytellers

The gift of parables is another way the elusive God comes to us. These weeks open us to the person of Jesus, but often in an oblique way. Now Wondering becomes our new Work. This is a *Parable*, one of the four genres in Godly Play®.

Getting Ready

Telling the Story of the Parable of the Good Shepherd

The Parable of the Good Shepherd is found in *The Complete Guide*, Volume 3, pages 77–86.

The Wondering

The Work

Remember to support this time with a wealth of resources.

The Feast

Spend this time preparing for the Feast for the gathering on the last lesson. If the Feast is to be the Eucharist for the retreat, consider the stories, the work and perhaps preparing an altar to receive some of the offerings of their work and reflection. The Feast itself can be as simple as bread and wine or as complete as a final meal together, planned and prepared by the participants.

The Dismissal

Lesson 6: Baptism, the Good Shepherd, and World Communion

(*The Complete Guide to Godly Play*, Vol. 3, 70–76 and Vol. 4, 91–98)

Lesson Overview

Both of these stories are part of *Liturgical Action* and are *Core Presentations*. They will each be told and then, at the end, the participants will place their Object Boxes in the circle.

Notes for Storytellers

We end here but as we learned in our first lesson on time, in our beginnings are our endings and in our endings are our beginnings. We are a changed people, flowing in the river of life as one body.

These two stories anchor us in this holy and sacramental life.

Getting Ready

As we get ready for this final lesson, the Storyteller will make sure that there is an open space on the opposite side of the circle.

Telling the Story of Baptism

Holy Baptism is found in *The Complete Guide*, Volume 3, pages 70–76. There will be no Wondering with this lesson. The Storyteller will leave this story out and move to the other side of the circle to tell the second story.

Telling the Story of the Good Shepherd and World Communion

The lesson on the Good Shepherd and World Communion is found in Volume 4, pages 91–98.

The Wondering

At the end of the World Communion, the wondering will include bringing all the other stories in our series to the circle.

The Work

The work today is getting ready for the Feast.

The Feast

If this series is the culmination of the retreat, the Feast can be one last, small, and intimate moment of Holy Communion, using wonderful bread and great wine or a full meal celebrating the time together.

This is your Feast. It is yours to imagine and create, the offering of this community newly constituted as a small part of the body of Christ.

The Dismissal

This sending out will be a very holy moment: not the end, only the beginning.

Course IV:

Coffee with Cream (Sunday Mornings)

Godly Play® can be part of adult faith-formation on Sunday mornings. Typically congregations offer a forty-five-minute to one-hour period for formation programs. In that time frame, it is possible to gather the circle, tell a story and have a period of wondering. In the remaining time, work can be done or the Feast prepared and shared. Alternatives might include a book discussion or a short work session using a project that might be completed over the period of the semester. With the addition of an introductory class that lays out the Godly Play® method and prepares adults for the series, this offering could be used in the traditional semester format of thirteen weeks or split into two six-week sessions. Class size can vary from very small (four or five) to quite large (twenty or more).

A conference room or regular classroom will be needed since the Godly Play® space will likely be reserved for children. There should be enough room for the adults to gather in a circle with the Storyteller. It is important to create a small focal shelf for the holy family and to have the option of chairs for adults who are not able to sit on the floor.

Desired Outcome

Course IV provides an alternative program to the more traditional didactic class format for adults. It also provides a vehicle for deepening relationships, introducing Godly Play® to the community, and bridging the gap between new members and long-term members.

Goals of the Storyteller and Participants

- *Gather:* to building a "good circle"
- *Storytelling:* to learn a new way to experience scripture and liturgy
- *Engagement:* to meet each other in new ways

Schedule

For the first six lessons, a simple morning schedule allows for a story, the wondering, and a short work lesson or a Feast time. The last six lessons allow only time for the story and wondering.

Room, Materials, and Resources

Space

For Course IV, a meeting room with chairs set in a circle and a place for the Storyteller are needed. If there is sufficient time, a Feast may be shared.

Materials and Resources

The stories will need to be secured for each lesson as well as food and drink for the Feast when there is time. And, if there is one available, don't forget a field trip to the church's Godly Play® space.

Lesson 1: Circle of the Church Year

(*The Complete Guide to Godly Play*, Vol. 2, 23–33)

Lesson Overview

This story is part of the genre we label *Liturgical Action* and is a *Core Presentation*. We begin with an orientation in time and encounter the unique nature of religious language as opposed to all the other languages of our culture—scientific, legal, economic, psychological, sociological, political, ethical, philosophical, technological, even the language of the marketplace—we discover the realm of a different kind of time, the rhythm of beginnings and endings, punctuated by an encounter with mystery, the elusive and hidden Holy One.

In this first class, help participants prepare for this encounter.

Notes for Storytellers

Because this is your first time together, allow time for introductions and an explanation of the course.

Welcome participants into the circle and spend a few minutes describing the sequence of events for each class. Invite each person to

briefly introduce himself or herself. Using the format you have chosen, describe the desired outcomes for the course and the class agenda. A short overview about the Godly Play® history and method, the lessons, getting ready, wondering, and other useful information found in this text or in *The Complete Guide* will help them prepare for the first lesson.

Getting Ready

In Godly Play®, children are encouraged to ready themselves; however, adults may need a little more help. When all participants have gathered, the Storyteller can invite everyone to get in a comfortable position, either in a chair or on the floor, and to close their eyes. For a minute or two, all are invited to breathe deeply, in and out. Breathing deeply brings oxygen into the body, lowering anxiety, releasing the tension we hold in our bodies all the way down to each cell. This also helps participants shift into a different kind of learning mode. Throughout this series of lessons, we will follow a similar pattern of getting ready for our story.

Begin with this meditation practice, allowing two full minutes, inviting everyone to sit comfortably, close their eyes, and place their right hand over their heart. Ring the bell or sound the bowl to begin. Breathing in and out through the nostrils, count softly: Breathe in 1,2,3,1 and breathe out 1,2,3,2, breathe in 1,2,3,3, breathe out 1,2,3,4 and breathe in 1,2,3,1 and breathe out 1,2,3,2, breathe in 1,2,3,3 and breathe out 1,2,3,4. *Keep the breath going, reminding them that when the mind starts wandering to just come back to the breath.* At two minutes, ring the bell or sound the bowl, signaling the end of the meditation. Listen to the sound until it can no longer be heard. Now we are ready.

Telling the Story of the Circle of the Church Year

Our first lesson is also Lesson 1 in *The Complete Guide*, Volume 2, and begins on page 23.

The Wondering

The Wondering questions are found on page 32 (p. 10 in the digital version of *The Circle of the Church Year*). At first the Wondering will be awkward. Adults often think there must be a correct answer or perhaps there is a trick to this Wondering. Silence can be unbearable. The

Storyteller must breathe and let the silence continue until someone is brave enough to respond. The good news is that they will get better and better at Wondering.

In this first lesson, some of our regular available time for Work has been used in the orientation.

The Work

When there is time, participants follow the normal schedule of work.

The Feast

If there is time, members will share prayers and the Feast.

The Dismissal

This is holy time, and each person will be sent off with a blessing from the Storyteller. See *The Complete Guide*, Volume 1, page 58 for thoughts about sending out into the world. The Storyteller can say something such as, "It was wonderful to have you here today."[54]

Lesson 2: Creation

(*The Complete Guide to Godly Play*, Vol. 2, 41–48)

Lesson Overview

As infants, we first orient in space and time. In scripture, we also orient in space and time. We begin with creation, out of nothing, first light, the impulse of energy—wave and particle. The beauty of beginning at the beginning allows for a graceful emptiness—we begin with nothing, but soon we find ourselves surrounded by wonder. With these two lessons, we are now ready; oriented in space and time, now it is time to get moving. Who are we and where are we going?

Notes for Storytellers

In the beginning, God created the heavens and earth....

It is like this in the human realm as well—from nothing but love, a child is born.

---

[54] Berryman, *The Complete Guide to Godly Play*, Vol. 1, 58.

We begin our second lesson with the story of Creation, gathering the community into the circle for the second time.

This is a *Sacred Story* and one of the *Core Presentations* in Godly Play®. (Remember the four genres include *Sacred Stories, Liturgical Action, Parables*, and *Silence*.)

Jerome Berryman reminds us: "With this lesson we begin to trace the elusive presence of the mystery of God in the story of God's People. We begin to play hide-and-seek with the Holy One and ask, 'What can we know of the Giver by the gift?'"[55]

Developmentally, a child journeys across a threshold called object permanence somewhere between one and two years. This milestone represents the ability to hold an object in one's mind, even when it is not in sight (or present through the other senses). This is the moment when games like "peekaboo" bring delight to child and parents alike—a special kind of play begins with this ability. It is interesting to note that although this ability is critical to the development of the frontal cortex, its value is often lost in the hyper-rational adult who says, "Seeing is believing." We have forgotten how to play.

We discover with the Creation story an opportunity to recover the delight of playing with the Creator who is hidden from view, yet present in the very creation that surrounds us. Our work with adults must undo and rediscover what is key to the Christian life. God fills all Creation, even when not apparently visible. Young children have far less trouble playing hide-and-seek in the time of wondering than adults. So, this is where we will start, remembering what we cannot see or prove, anchoring ourselves in space and the wonder of Creation.

Getting Ready

Remember to slow down and breathe deeply first.

When everyone is quiet and the Storyteller feels the rhythm of the room settling, it is time to begin. After the first few lessons, the Storyteller will begin to get a feel for the group. Some will come in ready to gather for the presentation of the story; others will bring a world of concerns and anxiety with them. Help the participants get ready by providing a few moments of centering themselves.

---

[55] Berryman, *The Complete Guide to Godly Play*, Vol. 2, p. 41; p. 1 in the digital version of Creation.

Telling the Story of Creation

Remember to be fully prepared, having practiced the story and the questions for wondering. The Creation Story is found in *The Complete Guide*, Volume 2, on pages 41–48.

The Wondering

Again, allow for the silences.

The Work

It is now time to shift the community from wondering to their work. With the children, the Storyteller invites each to leave the circle for their work, thus acknowledging that each is valued in the circle. We provide that same invitation to our adult participants—crossing the threshold and entering into the sacred space of the circle helps set the tone for the experience. Helping each one to begin their response by inviting them to leave the circle, allows for a quiet transition. Once the participants have engaged in their response to the story, the Storyteller and Doorperson are there for encouragement. See *The Complete Guide*, Volume 1, pages 53–58 for an overview.

The Feast

The Storyteller and Doorperson will serve as hosts for the first two lessons, modeling the hospitality of the servant's heart and the invitation to experience community through prayers and the Feast.

The Dismissal

And always, there is a graceful sending forth.

Lesson 3: The Great Family

(*The Complete Guide to Godly Play*, Vol. 2, 57–64)

Lesson Overview

As adults, we already know the desert is a dangerous place. We also think we know who we are. This story takes us on a journey that will test our willingness to leave what is familiar and comfortable. If Parker Palmer is right about the value in being disillusioned so that we might

be stripped of our illusions, this is where it begins. We are stripped down until we reach the time and place where God can come close. This is a *Sacred Story* and one of the *Core Presentations*.

Notes for Storytellers

I have always been amazed at how much adults like the desert box. Just like the children, they want to put their hands into the sand. This is a very powerful story. Don't rush, be mindful of transitions and set a pace that is marked by deliberate movement, intentional reflection and the occasional surprise that comes when insight is enacted.

Getting Ready

As always, take time to settle and breathe. By now, participants will look forward to this time with anticipation, not anxiety.

Telling the Story of the Great Family

The Complete Guide, Volume 2, page 57 provides background information and additional notes (p. 1 in the digital version of The Great Family). Always take your time with the preparation.

The Wondering

Wondering questions are on page 64 (p. 8 in the digital version of The Great Family). Let your own wondering and preparation expand the possibilities.

The Work

Remind participants that the stories are theirs to work with as well as the other options of writing, working with art materials, or simply sitting in quiet reflection.

The Feast

If there is time, the Feast can be offered and the prayers shared.

The Dismissal

Lesson 4: The Exodus

(*The Complete Guide to Godly Play*, Vol. 2, 65–72)

Lesson Overview

The People of God, this Great Family, found itself in a time and place of danger—they are slaves to power and seem helpless to seek a new way. Will freedom come? Are we prepared for the cost and the promise of freedom? This is a *Sacred Story* and part of the *Core Presentations*.

Notes for Storytellers

"God was with the People as they went out (the literal meaning of the word *exodus*) from slavery into freedom through the water. The People of God have looked back to this time to sustain them when God is hidden and they feel lost. For Christians, Baptism reawakens this event, especially when commemorated in the Easter Vigil... In these stories, we continue to evoke the People's experiences of God's elusive presence."[56]

Getting Ready

The class should be shifting into this posture automatically but it always helps to stop and breathe.

Telling the Story of the Exodus

The Story of the Exodus begins on page 65 of Volume 2 of *The Complete Guide*.

The Wondering

The wondering questions are on pages 71–72 (pp. 7–8 in the digital version of The Exodus), concluding with a taste of unleavened bread.

The Work

The great themes of captivity and freedom provide a rich opportunity for work to be done. Participants are already working on their

---

[56] Berryman, *The Complete Guide to Godly Play*, Vol. 2, p. 65; p. 1 in the digital version of The Exodus.

own stories, and these themes may be especially important to some of them. Remember we are tapping into more hidden aspects of our lives; sometimes this work evokes significant experiences from one's past.

The Feast

The Dismissal

Lesson 5: The Exile and the Return

(*The Complete Guide to Godly Play*, Vol. 2, 93–99)

Lesson Overview

"Abraham and Sarah traveled away from their home, a land where people thought that gods were in each thing—such as in the sky, in a river, or in a tree. The understanding that 'all of God might be everywhere' sustained Abraham and Sarah as they finally made their way to Canaan, where Isaac was born. And God was there.

"In this lesson, nearly the same arcing journey is taken by God's People, but this time in the opposite direction. And once again, they discover the same truth—God's presence is not here or there but everywhere, waiting. To be found. To find us."[57]

Notes for Storytellers

We return to the desert and another long journey. Apparently breaking the patterns that lead us into bondage is not easy. For the third week in a row—back to that desert. This is a *Sacred Story* and one of the *Core Presentations*.

In this series for adults, we move quickly through the *Sacred Stories*, leaving many out. One day, if we have been successful in creating an environment where adults experience Godly Play® as spiritual practice, we can move through all the stories. Our goal in this series is to give them enough to create an interior shift and a longing for more.

---

[57] Berryman, *The Complete Guide to Godly Play*, Vol. 2, p 93; p. 1 in the digital version of The Exile and the Return.

Now we prepare to face the truth of our lives. We are getting ready to share our own stories.

Getting Ready

The rhythm is set. Today we return to the desert one final time.

Telling the Story of the Exile and the Return

This story is found on page 93 of Volume 2 of *The Complete Guide*.

The Wondering

The Wondering is found on page 98 of Volume 2 (p. 6 in the digital version of The Exile and the Return).

The Work

The Feast

The Dismissal

Lesson 6: The Holy Family

(*The Complete Guide to Godly Play*, Vol. 3, 20–26)

Lesson Overview

Godly Play® has the potential to shift one from the *existential vacuum* (emptiness) to a place of *existential meaning* (full integration). Jerome Berryman says it this way:

> The holy family is the *matrix*—the Latin word for womb—out of which new life comes. This story is the story of the re-creation of the universe, Christ's incarnation changes everything.
> The axis of life in the Christian tradition is birth-death-rebirth.[58]

The holy family is the pivot around which the whole system moves.

---

[58] Berryman, *The Complete Guide to Godly Play*, Vol. 3, p. 20; p. 1 in the digital version of The Holy Family.

Notes for Storytellers

The Holy Family is an *Enrichment Lesson* and also reflects *Liturgical Action*. For the children it is repeated each time there is a change of seasons. It is a reminder of the changing colors and the rhythm of seasons. The holy family sits in the center of the Focal Shelf in the Godly Play® space; "We find existential meaning in our lives, in the places into which we are born, through the network of these relationships. The 'answer' to life is not a propositional statement or verbal key. Instead of an answer, we find a 'home,' every day, in the midst of these relationships of love and creating."[59] We begin with this pivotal story. "The birth-death-rebirth axis is perceived through the naming of the holy family, and through the careful, respective moving of the figures. We, like the holy family, are invited to be co-creators in the biological, psychological, social, and spiritual spheres of life."[60]

Getting Ready

Telling the Story of the Holy Family

The Story is found in the *The Complete Guide*, Volume 3, pages 20–26.

The Wondering

The Wondering is found on page 26 (p. 7 in the digital version of The Holy Family).

The Work

The Feast

The Dismissal

---

[59] Berryman, *The Complete Guide to Godly Play*, Vol. 3, p. 20; p. 1 in the digital version of The Holy Family.

[60] Berryman, *The Complete Guide to Godly Play*, Vol. 3, pp. 20–21; pp. 1–2 in the digital version of The Holy Family.

Lesson 7: Advent and Christmas

(*The Complete Guide to Godly Play*, Vol. 3, 27–51)

Lesson Overview

Having already told the story of the holy family, we are now ready to move toward Bethlehem and arrive at the birth of Jesus and the lighting of the Christ Candle. The "pointing prophets," along with the holy family, the shepherds, and the Magi, guide us.

Jerome Berryman says, "Religious language gives order to our lives, asking us to find what is new and different in the sameness. Religious language is generative language: it calls us to be who we are really supposed to be, creatures who create. In this lesson, we are also trying to enter into mystery. We want to come as close to it as we can."[61] To do this, we cannot stand back and analyze or rationalize. That is a different kind of work suited more to mathematics and science. As we tell this story, we are also telling our own stories. Remember that these stories are also filled with wonder and mystery.

Notes for Storytellers

From *Sacred Stories* that helped shape identity, we now begin the journey that changes everything. It takes four weeks to get ready to enter into the Mystery of Christmas, but we will take that journey all at once. This is part of our *Liturgical Action* and an *Enrichment Presentation*. Currently the language and the experience of Christmas are captive to a culture of consumption and transaction. Our work is harder because we feel as if we know this story, but the story we know is nostalgic and trite, wrapped up in a bow but not in mystery. Recovering meaning and mystery of the whole Christian story will be the task for these next six weeks.

Getting Ready

---

[61] Berryman, *The Complete Guide to Godly Play*, Vol. 3, p. 35; p. 9 in the digital document Advent Compilation, which contains all of the Advent lessons.

Telling the Story of Advent and Christmas

The story is found in the *The Complete Guide*, Volume 3, pages 27–52. Also read A Children's Liturgy for Christmas, and the *Enrichment Lessons* of the Mystery of Christmas and Epiphany (pp. 52–69). We will be telling the whole story in this one session. It will take a little longer and, as you are comfortable, you can adapt relevant words and phrases from the *Enrichment Lessons* to the story.

The Wondering

There are no Wondering questions for this story. *Silence* is a most welcome companion to this story.

The Work

The Feast

The Dismissal

Lesson 8: Parable of the Good Shepherd

(*The Complete Guide to Godly Play*, Vol. 3, 77–86)

Lesson Overview

The primary sheep-and-shepherd parable of Jesus, recognized as authentic by many scholars, tells of the shepherd who searches for the one sheep that is lost and leaves the ninety-nine to do so. In this presentation, the gate is left open as the shepherd searches for the sheep, but you will also find that many of life's conflicts find meaning and resolution in the themes from Psalm 23 and John 10, also present in the lesson.

The term *parable* can have a wide meaning. This lesson is more of an identity statement of Jesus than a parable.

Notes for Storytellers

The gift of parables is another way the elusive God comes to us. These weeks open us to the person of Jesus, but often in an oblique way. Now Wondering becomes our new Work. This is a *Parable*, one of the four genres in Godly Play®.

Getting Ready

Telling the Story of the Parable of the Good Shepherd
> The Parable of the Good Shepherd is found in *The Complete Guide*, Volume 3, pages 77–86.

The Wondering

The Work

The Feast

The Dismissal

Lesson 9: The Faces of Easter I–VII

(*The Complete Guide to Godly Play*, Vol. 4, 32–63)

Lesson Overview
As we begin this lesson, we note that we prepare for the second great mystery, the mystery of Easter. Lent is the season of preparation for Easter. The Faces of Easter I–VII moves us toward the Mystery by presenting the stories of Christ's journey toward the cross and resurrection. The *Liturgical Action* of the Faces of Easter is a *Core Presentation*. The children spend the six weeks of Lent to hear the whole story. We will move through them all in today's lesson.

Notes for Storytellers
Telling the story this way seems so simple, and yet it ends back at the beginning, the re-creation of the universe. This lesson calls for much silence. Practice this lesson until you know it well. You will guide adults through a story they think they know, allowing this story to flower in unexpected ways. The potential for integrating all they have learned or thought of as separate and disconnected is great.

When done in a Godly Play® space, the children are invited during the Wondering to make these connections with objects in the room.

Enrich the experience by taking your time, inviting silence and encouraging connections to participants' own stories and memories.

Today, as Object Box stories continue to be offered during the work time, staying in the circle will take on an even more significant meaning as the Faces of Easter and the Object Box personal stories offer a sense of connection, a kind of side-by-side view. The flow of this lesson brings a new level of integration—the Story and our stories flow together. The theological themes align the personal and the profound, providing insight and a sense of unity.

Getting Ready

As always, bring your own quiet spirit to the circle.

Telling the Story of the Faces of Easter

The Story begins in *The Complete Guide* in Volume 4 on page 32 and continues through several lessons, ending on page 68.

The Wondering

The Wondering questions are found in Volume 4 of *The Complete Guide* on pages 35, 41, 46, 51, 56, 62, and 68. In the digital version they are found on pages 4, 10, 15, 20, 25, 31, and 37 of the download titled The Faces of Easter Compilation).

The Work

There will not be time for work with these final stories.

The Feast

Today and over the remaining lessons, there will be time for prayers only.

The Dismissal

Lesson 10: Knowing Jesus in a New Way

(*The Complete Guide to Godly Play*, Vol. 8, 80–131)

Lesson Overview

"The season of Easter (Eastertide) extends the experience of Easter Sunday for six weeks, but it also helps prepare for the coming of the

Mystery of Pentecost. This period is a transition between Jesus' earthly ministry and the coming of the Holy Spirit."[62]

Notes for Storytellers

Eastertide unfolds in doubt and confusion, then joy and wonder. The transformation of the disciples calls us to look in the mirror. Are we ready?

This is a big lesson to prepare for, and, like the Faces of Easter, is done over a series of weeks with the children. In church, we hear these stories from the three-year cycle of the Revised Common Lectionary but never experience them in this rhythmic sequence. It is a powerful conclusion to the Lent and Easter cycle, culminating with Pentecost. As always, it is important for the Storyteller and Doorperson to be ready.

Getting Ready

As always, we prepare with silence and a few moments of breathing deeply.

Telling the Story of Knowing Jesus in a New Way

This Story is found in *The Complete Guide*, Volume 8 beginning on page 80 and concluding on page 131 and in the digital version as Knowing Jesus in a New Way, Parts 1 to 7.

The Wondering

The Feast

Time is given for only prayers.

The Dismissal

---

[62] Berryman, *The Complete Guide to Godly Play*, Vol. 8, p. 124; p. 1 in the digital version of Knowing Jesus in a New Way, Part 7: Known by the Holy Spirit.

Lesson 11: The Greatest Parable

(*The Complete Guide to Godly Play*, Vol. 8, 32–62)

Lesson Overview

This lesson is the only one that can be presented without words. We will tell it with words, allowing the elusive presence of God to speak to everyone in the circle. The introduction and notes in the *The Complete Guide*, Volume 8 are very important. Preparing for this lesson will take time.

Jerome Berryman tells us:

> These lessons present Jesus' public ministry and the relation of his presence to the whole Christian language system. This is a parable, because Jesus is not a window through which God can be glimpsed passing by. Rather, Jesus is an embodiment of God in the frailty and finitude of a human being. Like a parable, Jesus' life hides as well as reveals. It hides and reveals both the divinity and humanity of Jesus, but also with grace, and to a lesser degree, the divinity and humanity in our lives as well.
>
> This is "The Greatest Parable" because Jesus is the source of parables. He is the "Parable Maker"; out of whole life comes our *Sacred Stories, Liturgical Action, and Silence*, as well as *Parables*. This lesson, therefore, needs to draw to itself and express the whole Christian language system as represented in the Godly Play® room.[63]

Notes for Storytellers

The goal of this presentation is to "allow the inexhaustible meaning and linguistic complexity of Jesus to shine through with a kind of deep simplicity that it is open to all of us."[64] If it is possible to use the Godly Play® space for this story, this would be the time to bring participants to the room to experience the whole language system.

---

[63] Berryman, *The Complete Guide to Godly Play*, Vol. 8, p. 32; p. 1 in the digital version, titled The Greatest Parable [the Presentation with Words, Part 1].

[64] Berryman, *The Complete Guide to Godly Play*, Vol. 8, p. 33; p. 2 in the digital version, titled The Greatest Parable [the Presentation with Words, Part 1].

We are almost at the ending of our time together, but as we know, we are now at the threshold of a new beginning. The end of this story offers just one wondering: *Now, I wonder what goes here. . . .*

Getting Ready

Telling the Story of the Greatest Parable

This story is found in *The Complete Guide*, Volume 8, beginning on page 32.

The Wondering

With just one question and the very contemplative moment that comes at the end of this story, the invitation to make a response in the time set aside for their work provides an opportunity to explore the whole room—to see what fills in the gaps of their experience in this course. Maybe they will want more. By this time, the circle and the tables will have become indistinguishable—we are part of the Great Family.

The Feast

Prayers only.

The Dismissal

Lesson 12: Baptism

(*The Complete Guide to Godly Play*, Vol. 3, 70–76)

Lesson Overview

This story is part of the genre we label *Liturgical Action* and is a *Core Presentation*.

Notes for Storytellers

We end here, but as we learned in our very first lesson on time, in our beginnings are our endings and in our endings are our beginnings. We are a changed people, flowing in the river of life as one body.

Getting Ready

As we get ready for this final lesson, the Storyteller will make sure that there is an open space on the opposite side of the circle.

Telling the Story of Baptism

Holy Baptism is found in *The Complete Guide*, Volume 3, pages 70–76. There will be no Wondering with this lesson. The Storyteller will leave this story out and move to the other side of the circle to tell the second story.

The Feast

This is your Feast, yours to imagine and create, the offering of this community newly constituted as a small part of the Body of Christ.

The Dismissal

This sending out will be a very holy moment but not the end, only the beginning

Bibliography

- Berryman, Jerome. *The Complete Guide to Godly Play.* Vols. 1–8. Denver: Morehouse Education Resources, 2012. (All materials also available digitally at: https://www.churchpublishing.org/complex/godlyplaydigital/

- ———. *Teaching Godly Play.* Denver: Morehouse Education Resources, 2012.

- ———. *Children and Theologians.* New York: Morehouse Education Resources, 2009.

- ———. *The Spiritual Guidance of Children.* New York: Morehouse Education Resources, 2013.

- Bass, Diana Butler. *Christianity After Religion.* San Francisco: HarperOne, 2012.

- Capon, Robert. *The Astonished Heart.* Grand Rapids: Eerdmans, 1996.

- ———. *The Supper of the Lamb.* New York: MacMillan, 1989.

- ———. *The Parables of the Kingdom.* Grand Rapids: Zondervan Publishing House, 1985.

- Crabtree, J. Russell. *Owlsight.* Columbus: Magi Press, 2012.

- Lewis, Thomas, Fari Amini, and Richard Lannon. *A General Theory of Love.* New York: Vintage Books, 2001.

- Liddell, Henry George, and Robert Scott. *A Greek-English Lexicon, on Perseus.* Eastford, CT: Martino Publishing, 2015.

- "OREGON: Marcus Borg named canon theologian at Trinity Cathedral in Portland." *Episcopal News Service*, July 17, 2009. http://www.episcopalchurch.org/library/article/oregon-marcus-borg-named-canon-theologian-trinity-cathedral-portland.

- Painter, Christine Valters and Betsey Beckman. *Awakening the Creative Spirit.* Harrisburg: Morehouse Publishing, 2010.

- Weber Christain Blue Cloth ¶ Appendix: Penny Yes

- Esquivel, Julia. *Prayers and Poems from the River Guatemalan.*

- Wilson, Edward O. *The Social Conquest.* New York: Liveright Publishing, 2012.

- ———. 2014. *The Meaning of Human Existence.* New York: Liveright Publishing, 2014.

Additional Resources

- Bible, New Revised Standard Version
- Book of Common Prayer (1979)
- The Hymnal 1982

Authors and Other Sources of Inspiration

This is a small selection of authors and poets whose work is accessible and provides a resource for transitions from the work/response time to table time. Feel free to choose your own favorite works and invite your participants to do the same. Some may even write their own, but others may have an offering of music or art.

- Bourgeault, Cynthia. *Mystical Hope: R. Steiner the New Theologian.* Boston: Cowley Publications, 2001.

- O'Donohue, John. *To Bless the Space Between Us.* New York: Doubleday, 2008.

- Oliver, Mary. *New and Selected Poems. Volume I: When Death Comes.* Boston: Beacon Press, 1992.

Appendix

Sample Materials

Figure 1: *Object Boxes*

Figure 2: *Object Boxes*

Figure 3: *Container and Bowl with Beads*

Figure 4: *Godly Play® Meditation Beads*

Figure 5: *Bowl of Beads and Meditation Beads*

I wonder

Figure 6: *Sample Materials in Container*

Figure 7: *Container, Beads, Books*

Figure 8: *Godly Play® Meditation Beads*